MW00513018

INSPIRATIONS BY COLLEEN

A New England Woman's Look at Cooking, Family and Life

Colleen L. Bruce

Disclaimer: The guidance, inspiration(s) or suggestions in this book should not take the place of counseling, a doctor's advice, or spiritual guidance. This publication is intended for pleasure and insight into Colleen's New England Kitchen and some of my experiences. Its intention is to inspire, share the perception and living out of my journey with God and others.

DEDICATIONS

I am thankful to my heavenly Father for His love and grace throughout the years. My husband, Michael whose confidence in and love for me has been a blessing beyond compare. To Kim and Dan for showing me your testimony of what a true walk, forgiveness, and trust in the Lord looks like, thank you. To Jessie, my heart and prodigal, and I love you all.

Michelle, there are no words adequate for the godsend you are to me, thank you for your obedience and love. Benjamin and Morgan, my whole – heart, what else can Nanny say? Paula, my editor, God bless you.

SECTIONS

INTRODUCTION

Welcome! I'm thrilled to share a bit of life here in New England. Our family settled in this area in the mid 1700s. In 2007 I wrote my first book, Colleen's New England Kitchen: Tried & True Recipes for Cooking & Life. For the next several years I would do pie making demonstrations and talks at libraries, stores, and other venues with much success throughout New England. This cookbook was a jumping off place, if you will, to the book I ultimately wanted to write, my memoir.

In 2014 after 30 years of recovery work and a much needed final boost at the time from the Celebrate Recovery Program, I wrote my life story. Lord's Hill: A Place Only God Could Save Me From by, Maggie Miller (penname). With the foreword by Dr. Aphrodite Matsakis. Lords Hill has been compared to Peyton Place based on another true story also in a small New Hampshire town. The premise for sharing my life story was to expose and stop the isolation, shame and ignorance that often surround PTSD (post traumatic disorder) and the search for God's truth.

To help society understand the fallout that can come with multi-generational abuse, trauma, mental illness, addiction and adultery. When we think about how many teens and adults are a product of their environment and instilled emotional and physical experiences, we always need to be mindful of our need to earnestly search out the God of the

Bible, as the ultimate Father, Healer, and Judge. This book is still available at WestBow Press, Amazon, and Barnes & Noble.

Although my life has been overshadowed at times with loss, abuse, addiction, and tragedy, I've also learned valuable lessons that money can't buy and death cannot take away. I am grateful to God for giving me the ability to glean from the people and events in my life: a strong work ethic, creative skills that have empowered me to make a living as well as learn how fragile life is, and often painful truths that come with reality. And it is by His grace that I am able to have humility and never give up my search for a better life.

In all these things and more I came from a family of wonderful cooks, hard workers, good gardeners, and story tellers, with quick wit, hot tempers and big hearts. I want to invite you into a little piece of my New England. Most of all I love God, people young and old, and life in general. I love to enrich the lives of others.

Thank you for allowing me the honor of sharing these things with you.

Colleen L. Bruce / (aka Maggie Miller)

SECTION ONE

My New England

I'd like to start off with a poem my oldest daughter wrote, which for many New Englander families depicts how we have felt for generations.

I Love...

By Kimberly Bruce Perkins

The sight of a deer in autumns late

The smell of venison on my plate

Mulling cider on the stove

Collecting shells in a cove

Eggs and bacon on a Sunday morn

Carving pumpkins and husking corn

Fickle weather and the changing tide

Meeting the dawn with matching stride

Making a living where you tread

Your greatest comfort being warm and fed

Knowing a servant of his land

That takes the earth by the hand

Pleasant evenings and mystic nights

Catching a glimpse of the Northern lights

A drafty barn housing a newborn calf

When it seems like daylight has been cut in half

Apple pie and banana bread

Warming bricks for the foot of your bed

Fireworks and the Fourth of July

Going to church and knowing why

Snow-covered mountains and a rocky coast

I love these things, but what I love the most

… Is New England

Traditions of the Seasons

SPRING

MARCH 1 – MAY 31

In March

Beverly McLoughland

The garden is brown;

The garden is bare;

Winter bellow

A double-dare

At Spring, who boldly,

Despite the chill,

Smacks the Big Bully

With a daffodil.

Mid March is the start of mud season. Roads are posted for heavy trucks with throaty roar and heavy loads. Those who have dirt dooryards sweep half of it back out one dustpan full at a time by late April. The sugar maple sap runs slow and then picks up its pace as warmer days of spring and the lingering cold nights of winter lose their mighty grip. The harmony of cold and warmth touch tree, brook, and land giving hope of blossoms and new things to come.

Easter time is when I take down my Christmas cards, I always figured if so many people took the time to remember during the celebrated season of Jesus' birth, I should leave them up until the season of celebration for His resurrection.

Each year before dinner is served we have a family member, friend or our daughter Kim herself read the Easter Tribute she wrote as a young girl.

An Easter Tribute

By: Kimberly Bruce

A life that started in a virgin's womb

And ended up buried in a borrowed tomb

Who was resurrected three days after the fact

With the tomb empty and the stone rolled back

Today we're celebrating Jesus' death

Because for us He gave His last breath

God's only loss was when Jesus died on the cross

But He gave Him up because He loved mankind

No matter how faithless or how blind

The only One put into this world with a pure heart

Died so God and us would never part

Accept the gift and your debt is paid

The greatest sacrifice has already been made

God's precious son has been slain

To free you of your bondage and pain

We are all sinful and we all fail

But Jesus was imprisoned to pay our bail

Abandoned, beaten, and abused

A bond with paradise is what He fused

He was condemned by the high priest

Was worth the most but regarded as least

He carried His own cross all alone

So for your sins He could atone

Full of loneliness and despair He turned the other cheek

Just to be slapped by the evil and weak

The Greatest King treated like dirt

He had more sympathy for others than for His own hurt

All they could do was curse and mock

The Shepherd brought down by His flock

But He makes our sins look snow-white

In the darkness a ray of light

His faithfulness has been shown, it has been seen

We simply ask and our slate is wiped clean

The thorns were sharp and the whips did sting

But He died a Holy King

Hated by many, but by the wisest adored

Seated at the right hand of the Lord

Drink the wine and eat the bread

Because of you His blood was shed

The perfect, loving man forsaken

So our burdens could be taken

Not because of our righteousness,

But because God loved us so

The only reason He could let His only son go

Now our destiny can be sealed

Our chains broken and the wounds healed

So let's thank the Father for the Son;

For a life well lived and a job well done…

Longer, warmer and sunnier days give broody hens cause to lay more eggs. Spring greens and rhubarb seem to burst out of the ground over night and harvest time seems short for them. Regular garden planting time by tradition is usually Memorial Day weekend, when the last signs of frost are gone over hill and vale.

Ephraim

By Charles Churchill
Early Settlement & Other Poems

He came alone on May and took the house
And land that Louis left when Louis left to find another life.
A drafty place with pump and stove, and sagging cot,
It gave him shelter from the sun and rain, and little else.

Before that summer passed, we think he must have known why
Louis left, with land so scant and soil so close to ledge. He
couldn't grow enough to keep him through the winter months.

We saw him straining in his field and talked among ourselves,
as neighbors often do. And one of us with larger house and
work for all, took Ephraim in, and kept him on to work his
way, a Christian board and room.

The mother of the house, as ever, mother to them all, would
view him later as she would a father grown too old to keep his

home, but having hands to help her fold her clothes. Or hold her skein when she was balling yarn.

When even that was more than he could do, there came a dream that had no end. They gave him space within their family lot, and chiseled; FATHER EPHRAIM on his stone and nothing more.

Memorial Day parades are traditional in villages and towns. Reverent onlookers cover their hearts with pride, while men in uniform from various branches of the military march with pride. Floats, bicycles, baby strollers and cars are adorned with red, white and blue and the American flag flies high and low as the marching band sends an echo to heaven. At the end all the children run to the local schoolhouse or store wherever the speaker's podium is, and free ice cream or popsicles are passed out to all the children.

My first husband, David Bruce, who was a Vietnam Veteran and served in the Air Force Reserves until his death in 1996 was frequently the speaker for the Memorial Day celebration. This is his speech from 1989.

Memorial Day Speech

On Memorial Day whenever someone approaches the speaker's platform in many cities and towns, the audience will say, "Where did the speaker come from?" For the past few years, with the exception of last year, the Memorial message in Milton / Milton Mills has been given by someone that has lived in town.

I believe that…if you know the people in town perhaps you know what people need to hear. Many Memorial Day speakers will focus on the current problems of the day, and worldly threats to our way of life. I cannot tell you of the potential dangers in the Middle East and the Panama Canal Zone. You all know these dangers. We cannot help in those situations…we elect representatives to Congress, hoping they will face these issues.

What I can tell you, are things we can do something about. We can remind our friends, neighbors and…especially our children the true meaning of patriotism. The children in the schools today are the persons that will be the leaders of our communities, in a few years. They must be taught that the American Flag is the symbol of freedom throughout the world. Teachers in school should tell their students about the men from this town who have fought in all the wars our country has been engaged in, fighting to make this country… the land of the free.

When the children read of the historic Battle of Bunker Hill, they should be told, a man from Milton, NH was there. Also a man from Milton was with George Washington that winter at Valley Forge. Our area can boast that the last surviving man of the Revolutionary War lived across the river in Acton, Maine. The State of Maine had a day of celebration for this veteran, Ralph Farnum. The President of The United States met Mr. Farnum to pay respects to this veteran.

When history teachers tell their students of the war in the Pacific…the fall of Bataan and the infamous death march by the American prisoners of war, they should be told a man from Milton Mills, NH was in that march. Walking through hundreds of miles of jungle…and survived and returned home. Memorial Day is a day everyone should recall, remember and respect the heroes that died at places with strange sounding names like Anzio, Pork Chop Hill and Ho Chi Minh Trail.

There are over four hundred veterans living in Milton and Milton Mills. Every year the American Legion decorates the graves of over three hundred veteran heroes as a symbol that they will not be forgotten. Today, we the veterans who have served and survived…salute and honor those veterans that made the supreme sacrifice. In closing I'd like to read a short poem.

David K. Bruce Vietnam war 1970

Patriotism

Has it been over 200 years?

How the time seems to fly,

Or was it a few weeks ago

When Ralph Farnum was walking by?

He walked down this country road

As he had many times before,

Telling tales of the Revolution

To the folks at the General Store.

Our town doesn't change too much,

And perhaps we shouldn't care

As long as we have a certain bond

That country people share.

At the bridge, when the bugle sounds

Folks may feel a chill. I know

They'll hear taps sound, on Acton Ridge,

And an echo in the Salmon Falls below.

What causes that sudden chill?

Is there a fever in the crowd?

I hope that it's contagious,

It's something that makes you proud...

It's Patriotism!

David Kenneth Bruce

Memorial Day – Milton Mills, NH

May 30, 1989

My mentor for my first cookbook, Charlie Churchill was a great friend and father figure. He wrote a book of poetry that was so visual you went to the places he talked about and knew his characters like family and old friends. Here is one of many of my favorites.

First Settlement

By Charles Churchill

Beyond the mill, across the bridge, old roads meander to the farther hills. And some grow dim then vanish in the shade of trees. In younger days I walked these roads and found our early living place. Old cellar holes where toes and fingers found the daily things, of other lives beneath the autumn leaves, dull glass and such to fill our downtown shelves.

Off to the side of wooden lanes, and old homes are hid and hard to see, except in spring when scent of rose or lilac bloom, lies close to sunken stones and shows the line of walls. Here lived those whose lives turned narrow in the mold, of all the world they knew. Their neighbor's hand was the dearest hand to hold for all of life. The young, the old, the souls who breathed this air, it seems they still remain to haunt me there.

SUMMER

JUNE 1 – AUGUST 31

Paul Harvey's 1978 'So God Made a Farmer' Speech

"Hello, Americans," he barked. "This is Paul Harvey!

My husband, Michael Hickey, one of God's chosen farmers.

Here's the text of his (Paul Harvey) speech, made newly famous - during the Super Bowl:

So God Made a Farmer

And on the 8th day, God looked down on his planned paradise and said, "I need a caretaker." So God made a farmer.

God said, "I need somebody willing to get up before dawn, milk cows, work all day in the fields, milk cows again, eat supper and then go to town and stay past midnight at a meeting of the school board." So God made a farmer.

"I need somebody with arms strong enough to rustle a calf and yet gentle enough to deliver his own grandchild. Somebody to call hogs, tame cantankerous machinery, come home hungry, have to wait lunch until his wife's done feeding visiting ladies and tell the ladies to be sure and come back real soon -- and mean it." So God made a farmer.

God said, "I need somebody willing to sit up all night with a newborn colt. And watch it die. Then dry his eyes and say, 'Maybe next year.' I need somebody who can shape an ax handle from a persimmon sprout, shoe a horse with a hunk of car tire, who can make harness out of haywire, feed sacks and shoe scraps. And who, planting time and harvest season, will finish his forty-hour week by Tuesday noon, then, pain'n from 'tractor back,' put in another seventy-two hours." So God made a farmer.

God had to have somebody willing to ride the ruts at double speed to get the hay in ahead of the rain clouds and yet stop in mid-field and race to help when he sees the first smoke from a neighbor's place. So God made a farmer.

God said, "I need somebody strong enough to clear trees and heave bales, yet gentle enough to tame lambs and wean pigs and tend the pink-combed pullets, and will stop his mower for an hour to splint the broken leg of a meadow lark. It had to be somebody who'd plow deep and straight and not cut corners. Somebody to seed, weed, feed, breed and rake and disc and plow and plant and tie the fleece and strain the milk and replenish the self-feeder and finish a hard week's work with a five-mile drive to church.

"Somebody who'd bale a family together with the soft strong bonds of sharing, who would laugh and then sigh, and then reply, with smiling eyes, when his son says he wants to spend his life 'doing what dad does.'" So God made a farmer...

In New England, as with many other locations, farmers do not have the time to enjoy the long lazy days of summer or fuss about the "dog days" of August heat. Instead they are worrying about either too much rain or a summer drought. Hail storms that damage crops and pests both furry and flying, and making hay in between storms for winter feed.

July is best known for parades, fireworks and good food. Cookouts and frequent day trips with picnic baskets in tow are a summertime tradition to our many lakes and seacoast areas. Fruits and vegetables begin ripening on the vines and enjoyed within hours of picking. The abundance serves as a start of storage and canning for winter consumption and later satisfaction of the work of one's own hands.

Fourth of July is still celebrated in every community and is only over shadowed in some places by the lack of understanding of America's foundation and the celebration of her independence in 1776. History is there to serve us, lest we forget all that has been forged before for us, by lives that faced their own challenges in generations past.

August beckons September with the full maturity of root vegetables that winter over and provide holiday décor. The first of many country fairs are underway and the excitement and preparation for the larger ones have already seen months of preparation. Farmers, Grangers, 4-H, and other civic organizations, as well as children and adults of all ages display with pride their labors of love in hopes of a blue ribbon or best of show.

FALL

SEPTEMBER 1 – NOVEMBER 30

In the fall of the year New England is bursting with brilliant colors that span for miles across lakeshores, mountains, hillsides, and wooded lanes. Bright oranges, deep reds, and various yellows with slight brown streaks adorn the dancing leaves of maple, birch, beech, dogwood and oak. It's their grand finale after the other seasons have passed. With the hope for new life in spring, and summer shade and dancing limbs that memorize us and cause us to think of other days.

Juicy apples that look like red globes hang heavy on bent limbs as school children and families fill bags for apple pies and warm applesauce. Every child knows his own harvest and with an eager watchful eyes make sure teacher and parent alike give him back his own. Packing houses bring in migrant workers to help harvest the apples that will be put in cold storage for winter sales and keeping. In later fall the sweeter ones nipped by trumpet frost, make sweet the tartness of early crops and make the best cider.

Nights are often hot and humid during harvest season. We lie in bed, close to an open window, and watch the heat lightening dance across the further sky. Some nights there are beautiful electric storms and barely a drop of rain will fall. Sometimes during a heavy rain thunder claps will be so loud the house will shake just before God opens the heavens.

Pumpkins, gourds and Indian corn adorn porches and tabletops, while cornstalks line fence posts and the entrance to our homes. Halloween with trick - treating for candy and other sweet snacks excites the scariest of ghosts and witches as well as super heroes and princesses! Pumpkin carving is a gooey delight with seeds for roasting and later soggy treats for pasture cows. Sugar pumpkins have sweeter darker flesh and, cooked just right, make for pies fit for a king.

THE PUMPKIN

John Greenleaf Whittier

Ah! On Thanksgiving Day,
When from East and from West,
From North and from South
Come the Pilgrim and guest,
When the gray-haired New Englander
Sees round his board
The old broken links
Of affection restored
When the care-wearied man
Seeks his mother once more,
And the worn matron smiles
Where the girl smiled before,
What moistens the lip
And brightens the eye?
What calls back the past
Like pumpkin pie?
Oh-fruit loved of boyhood-
The old days recalling,
When wood-grapes were purpling
And brown nuts were falling!
When wild, ugly faces
We carved in its skin,
Glaring out through the dark
With a candle within!

When we laughed round the corn-heap,
With hearts all in tune,
Our lantern moon,
Telling tales of a fairy
Who traveled like steam,
In a pumpkin-shell coach,
With two rats for her team!

Thanksgiving Comes

We have two traditions in our home on Thanksgiving. I put white tablecloths over sheets of plastic on the dinner tables, as there's usually a crowd. And I put a couple colored permanent markers on each, so every person can write their name, the date and most importantly what they are thankful for. For years to come we look back over those we've loved and lost and those who have touched our lives.

The second tradition is to read Abraham Lincolns Thanksgiving Proclamation written in 1863. If we do not know what Thanksgiving means beyond a hefty meal and a prelude to Christmas, we've missed the whole point.

Thanksgiving Proclamation

...It is the duty of nations as well as of men, to own their
dependence upon the overruling power of Go, to confess
their sins and transgressions, in humble sorrow, yet with
assured hope that genuine repentance will lead to mercy and
pardon; and to recognize the sublime truth, announced in the
Holy Scriptures and proven by all history, that those nations
*only are blessed whose **God** is the **Lord**.*

...We know that, by His divine law, nations like individuals are subjected to punishments and chastisements in this world. May we not justly fear that the awful calamity of civil war, which now desolates the land, may be but a punishment, inflicted upon us, for our presumptuous sin, to the needful end of our national reformation as a whole People?. We have been the recipients of choicest bounties of Heave. We have been preserved, these many years, in peace and prosperity. We have grown in numbers, wealth and power, as no other nation has ever grown. But we have forgotten God.

*We have forgotten the gracious hand which preserved us in peace and multiplied and enriched and strengthened us; and we have vainly imagined, in the deceitfulness of our hearts, that all these blessings were produced by some superior wisdom and virtue of our own. Intoxicated with unbroken success, we have become too self-sufficient to feel the necessity of redeeming and preserving grace, too proud to pray to the **God** that made us!*

*It has seemed to me fit and proper that **God** should be solemnly reverently and gratefully acknowledged as with one heart and one voice by the whole American people. I do, therefore, invite my fellow citizens, in every part of these United States, and also those who are at sea and those sojourning in foreign lands, to set apart and observe the last Thursday of November as a Day of Thanksgiving and Praise to our beneficent **Father** who dwells in the heavens.*

By Abraham Lincoln

Fall is a time when God prepares the earth and us for a season of rest and letting go. In the meantime we take in the splendor of warm days and cool nights. Crackling woodstoves take the chill off cold fingertips and toes. As simmering mincemeat and hearty soups go wafting through the air to a chilly nose!

WINTER

DECEMBER 1 – FEBRUARY 28

All that is left is the brown and grays of fall for another year, and the brighter colors have blown away. The nights are twice as long, as darkness starts to fall right around suppertime. Woodstoves burn around the clock and time is spent relaxing on Sunday mornings from labors the previous three seasons. Reflection come easy and thoughts for the days ahead as Christmas begins to fill the conscious mind.

Time is spent most evenings filling out Christmas cards and wrapping gifts. The first weekend after Thanksgiving we gather again to trim the Christmas tree and happily deck each bough with ropes of gold and silver strands. While soft winter winds blow outside, reflections of the past set every tree from years past apart. Christmas for me is a child's face, peeking through the banisters at the magic everywhere. But, more important, and best of all, it's the blessing of Jesus' birth.

It's a time to cheerfully sing over and over, O Little Town of Bethlehem.

Christmas Traditions in New England

It's common for many families to get their Christmas tree the first weekend after Thanksgiving. For the family to gather once again and enjoy Thanksgiving leftovers while adorning the tree. In our home Christmas music is playing in the background, and the littlest child is held up by Papa to put the Christmas angel on the tree top. The tone is set to start watching Christmas movies almost nightly, and reading books and stories associated with the season. Cookies, candy and gingerbread making are in full swing. We make Christmas sleighs with candy canes, and believe some of the traditions about them. The J-shape stands for Jesus, and the peppermint flavor represents the hyssop that was used in the Bible for purifying. The white stripes represent His purity, and the red stripes are for the blood He shed on the cross.

Our Christmas trees are usually evergreen, Scotch pine, and balsam fir. We use the evergreens trees for wreaths and garlands which in some cultures represent eternal life. The modern Christmas trees originated in western Germany; which were introduced into England in the early 19th century. Victorian trees were decorated toys, candies, popcorn strings, and small gifts. Some of these same traditions stand today in many homes, also including tinsel, gold beads and colored lights adorn the trees in our New England homes.

For generations we have made paper chains from strips of colored paper hooked together with glue. Blown glass ornaments were introduced for sale in Britain and the United States as early as 1870's, also created were decorations made from tinsel, and cast lead beads. Also traditional to our home is popcorn and cranberries strung together on fine white cotton thread. Shorter strands are made to adorn center pieces. These naturally beautiful delights make good winter food for birds, and other tiny creatures when Christmas is over.

We always use the traditional tinsel, which was once banned by the government because it contained lead, and is now made of plastic. We gingerly separate the fine strands for a perfectly shaped glittering adornment all the way around the tree.

The sweetest and dearest part of Christmas is the Christ Child.

Jesus' Birth Foretold;

26 Now in the sixth month the angel Gabriel was sent from God to a city in Galilee called Nazareth, 27 to a virgin [a]engaged to a man whose name was Joseph, of the [b]descendants of David; and the virgin's name was [c]Mary. 28 And coming in, he said to her, "Greetings, [d]favored one! The Lord [e]is with you." 29 But she was very perplexed at this statement, and kept pondering what kind of salutation this was. 30 The angel said to her, "Do

not be afraid, Mary; for you have found favor with
God. [31] And behold, you will conceive in your womb and bear
a son, and you shall name Him Jesus. [32] He will be great and
will be called the Son of the Most High; and the Lord God
will give Him the throne of His father David; [33] and He will
reign over the house of Jacob forever, and His kingdom will
have no end." [34] Mary said to the angel, "How [f]can this be,
since I [g]am a virgin?" [35] The angel answered and said to
her, "The Holy Spirit will come upon you, and the power
of the Most High will overshadow you; and for that
reason the [h]holy Child shall be called the Son of God. [36] And
behold, even your relative Elizabeth has also conceived a son
in her old age; and [i]she who was called barren is now in her
sixth month. [37] For [j]nothing will be impossible with
God." [38] And Mary said, "Behold, the [k]bondslave of the
Lord; may it be done to me according to your word." And the
angel departed from her. Luke1:26-38

Then Christmas is over and the expectation of a new year lingers, only a few days away. January brings hours of time to ponder deeper thoughts and pack up fall and Christmas décor and make the pilgrimage up the tiny attic stairs. It's bitter cold up there, so, Valentines' Day decorations are passed down to store in a spare bedroom as it is only weeks away. The reds and pinks and the symbol of the heart give a tiny lift to a solemn winter mind. Thoughts of love and special times are shared by most. Nevertheless, we are glad to see the long dreary days of February go. March with its longer days brings hope of the coming spring. Winter has given time for the earth and all that inhabits it to rest for busier days and the seasons to come.

Stories to Warm the Heart and Make You Chuckle!

Marion (Grammy) Bruce

Grammy Bruce

My mother-in-law Marion Bruce was a short stocky woman, in her seventies with thinning gray hair, better known as Gram or Grammy Bruce by all who knew and loved her. I can still see her bowed legs rocking her back and forth ungracefully as she moved quickly about the kitchen. She owned an old cape style farmhouse, better known as "over home" by her and her family. Mother of five, widowed in her fifties and a retired factory worker, Gram gave unselfishly to her family, friends and neighbors most of her life.

You could see a bright spark of enthusiasm in her deep blue eyes, as she'd hang up the phone to head out the door on one of her many charitable missions for a less fortunate soul. She didn't live for fanfare or drape herself in fancy clothes. The only time she really dressed up was for a Clementine's concert, a singing group that she belonged to, which was one of the only luxuries in life that she afforded herself. Her usual attire was an old house dress or knit slacks and cotton top which usually sported some of that day's menu. No, her ego and all that she stood for was attached to the Lord.

Her toothless smile seemed to extend to her large soft ears that slightly protruded from the sides of her head. She loved singing hymns as she was scurrying about the house or sat crocheting. I was married to her eldest son, David, and during my first pregnancy I was ill most of the time. Many days my husband took me "over home" while he worked, for Gram to take care of me. It was during the winter and she'd have the woodstove going full bore; we used to joke that it made the floor underneath it so hot you could fry an egg on it. I'd lay most of the day on a comfy old cot that was pushed against the inside parlor wall, nestled down in layers of old worn bedding and one of Gram's oversized nightgowns.

I can still remember the smell of the damp dirt cellar that seeped between the squeaky old floor beneath me, the smell of Gram's stale coffee breath on the clothes that surrounded me blending with what was cooking in the kitchen and the smell of cats and her old dog, Girl. The best by far, but too few, Christmas Eves of my life were spent at her home. Her birthday was on Christmas Eve, and all the families would gather, as well as extended family and friends. We'd sing carols and eat her traditional chicken stew, and the kitchen would be filled with a potluck assortment big enough to feed Cox's Army had it come by.

Three short years later the ravages of Alzheimer's consumed her mind, and five years after that my husband died. I still pray his death was unknown to her. The last time I saw her at the nursing home she was holding a baby doll with what looked like a permanent grin on her face staring into glory. At her funeral six months later, after numerous testimonies that spanned generations, we sang her the rest of the way into glory with tears of happiness streaming down every face.

What a wonderful gift when the memory of love and time is given from the heart. This was Grammy Bruce. I learn from her, it is in the heart where the richest and most valuable treasures of life exist.

This is a true story, around 1931, as told by James Welch, former sheriff of Carroll County, NH. The tin-peddler Charles Hall was a relative of my fraternal grandmother, Frances Wilson.

Jeanette

A tin peddler named Charles Hall from Newmarket, NH, used to stay with Oliver Brown when he came through Ossipee, NH. Oliver lived alone on Brown's Ridge, and did his own cooking. Hall was a man who liked plenty of good things to eat, something he didn't often get when he stayed with Oliver. He would say to Oliver, "I shall be here a week from Saturday to stay with you. Be sure to have plenty of good beef steak when I come."

So, one time when he came, Oliver told him that he had something cooked up ahead and he had plenty of good beef steak. They had supper and Hall praising the beef steak, said, he'd never tasted better, and hoped he'd have some more for breakfast. Oliver cooked up some the next morning, and again Hall praised it.

Then Oliver said to him, "Well Hall, do you know where I got that beef steak?" Hall said no. "Well." Said Oliver, you know my old mare, Jeanette. That was a piece of her." Hall went outdoors and tried to get sick. Oliver came out and said, "T'aint no use Hall. She never backed one step when she was alive, and as sure as the sun will rise, she won't back now."

The next story pretty much tells the mindset of New Englanders, especially years ago.

Old Fred

"Just when you thought you might be a native."

One day old Fred sat puffing his pipe on the porch of the country store, when along came Dave; who was a newcomer to this small New England town, who'd been living there about forty years. As Dave approached the steps, he couldn't help but ask old Fred a haunting question. "Old Fred, I know I'm not a native, but all my kids were born here, don't that make them natives?"

Old Fred paused for a moment, pulled out his corn cob pipe that was wedged between his teeth and said, "Well I'll tell ya, son it's like this, just because your cat has kittens in the oven, it don't make em' biscuits!"

You Can't Put Running Shoes on a Work-Horse

My grandmother and my great-grandmother as they used to say, "Mostly worked around home." But for extra money they'd sometimes clean for people who could afford some outside help. They also took in laundry (that was washed and ironed by hand), boarders and made butter and salves to sell. I was raised by my maternal grandmother and at very young age I was helping her when she went out to clean, and had my first paying job at thirteen.

You never saw either of them without an apron on and I followed suit starting at eleven years old and still wear one every day. And I don't remember ever seeing either of them in a pair of high heeled shoes. However, when I was about nineteen years old I'd decided I wanted to go to the city to work. It was about 20 miles away and had a population of 14,000 people at the time, compared to our population of 350 it was quite an adventure. I landed a job at one of the big department stores.

My first day on the way out of town nothing would do, but I had to show off my fancy dress and high heeled shoes. I thought I'd get a coffee and show off to all the local road crew and lumber mill workers who were there for morning break. It was my first real experience in high heeled. As I went to step down into the area where people sat and drank coffee, I fell off my right heel and landed backwards into the Road Commissioners lap!

I could have died from embarrassment and the room filled with snickers and chuckles. He grabbed me with his big strong hands around the waist. As he stood me back on my feet he said, "What's the matter girl? Don't you know you can't put running shoes on a work- horse?"

Phyllis L. Morrill my Nana, and I

To a Wild Rose

One Christmas when I was about five, I wanted more than anything, to give my grandmother a present, something special, from just me. Christmas was and still is my favorite time of the year. Usually, I could talk Nana into letting me start decorating for Christmas right after Halloween! The older she got, the faster she gave in. In the late fall, when the big Sears and Spiegel Christmas catalogs came, Nana would let us kids pick out one special gift each.

She never told us what we could have. We never picked a really expensive gift, because we knew she couldn't afford much. But it was exciting to sit on the living room floor and dream. I'd go through the catalogs over and over again. One day I decided I wanted to do something for her, so I went on a mission to find something in the house to give Nana for Christmas. It had to be new. I was close to my grandmother and she was the only mother I ever remembered having. I slept in her room with her until she died when I was sixteen. When I was little she'd rub my back and sing to me until I'd settled down and Colleen fell asleep.

Just as I was starting to get a little discouraged with my search, I spotted it. On the back of Nana's bureau, hidden behind many other things was a dusty, but brand-new box of To a Wild Rose powder from Avon. Running into the kitchen where she was cooking, I forced myself to sit down quietly at the table. After numbing around for a few minutes, I said,

"Nana, are you going to use that box of To a Wild Rose Powder that's on your bureau?"

Cheerfully, she said, "No. Would you like it?" Yelling, as I ran out of the kitchen, "I can have it, I can really have it!" Quickly, I went into her room and grabbed it. Then I crawled under the dining room table to wrap it, where I was sure she wouldn't see me. Christmas mornings are the fondest memories I have of living with Nana. This one was the best. It was about giving her my gift. Excitedly, as she opened it, my hands were squeezed into tight fists against the sides of my face. I looked like I was going to explode!

She removed the last piece of wrapping paper looking genuinely surprised. Looking happily surprised, an expression I rarely saw over the years, she said, "To a Wild Rose powder! How did you know, baby doll (what she used to call me), I needed some powder?" To use one of her expressions, "I felt like a million dollars, only half spent." Many years later, when she was gone, I reflected back on that Christmas morning. An aching in my heart consumed me when I thought of her and the hard life she'd lived. My eyes welled up with tears. This Christmas memory would become one of many, causing me to grieve the loss of my grandmother, many times over. Years later, I would understand that resentment, anger and fear were directly related to the feelings of rejection and abandonment during my younger years and had affected most of my family.

Water, Water, Water!

Nana Morrill bought the farm where I grew up after my mother's death. It had a very shallow well, and was located quite a ways from the house, down over a small hill, and believe it or not next to a brook; but the well was always going dry. Late spring, and summer into fall water was scarce, especially in summer I bathed more outside then in.

It was a ritual for over thirteen years growing up there, for us to go to the river over town or up to the lake, in Sanbornville, about 2 miles from home to take our baths. Right after supper was cleaned up, Nana would holler, "Come on kids! Get your bathing suits on, get a bar of soap and shampoo and don't forget to bring a towel, you've got to get your baths taken!" Today, as it probably was in those days too, it would be against the law to do this in a public body of water.

Many times when she knew a good sized rain storm was coming, we'd bathe outside. The water would run off the roof like a faucet, so we'd put on our bathing suits and take turns washing up under the eaves. In the fall water was heated on the kitchen stove for sponge baths, and washing our hair in the kitchen sink. It was hauled just like it was in the summer from an outside faucet at my aunt's house over town; to water the animals, wash dishes and flush the toilet.

Not a drop was ever wasted, the sponge bath water, dish pan water and every other drop that didn't have to go down the drain was used to flush the toilet. If you got caught wasting water, you got the razor strap or a tongue lashing from my grandmother you wouldn't soon forget!

Pathways

By Charles Churchill

The woods are full of rain from overnight,

And I have left my sleep this day to see

Soft weep of bough, new green of leaf, and now

A path I walked so many dawns ago

In woods like these I cannot know for sure

Where life and dreams diverge or where they meet

Or where I may have gone before my sleep...

Early Settlement & Other Poems

By Charles Churchill

The Women that Help Shape My Life

Back Row: My Aunts, Goldie, Dodie, My Mother
and Aunt Colleen. Second Row: My Nana Morrill
and My Great Grandmother, Abby Grant

Milton Mills, NH

Many folks today do not know what the Grange Organization is all about. It was established in the 1870's as a non-profit by members called the Patrons of Husbandry, a farmers' organization that had been formed for social and cultural purposes. It encouraged families to band together, to promote the economic and political well-being of the community and agriculture.

Can't Ring a Hog that Roots for a Living

My Nana Morrill loved the Grange. Against the Grange rules, I started attending meetings at the age of 5, at the time membership age was 13 for junior Grange. For over 25 years she was the janitor. During the summer months into early fall, Nana ran Saturday morning coffee hour and the thrift shop, which was located in a large room in the back of the old hall. People would donate clothes for the thrift shop and if any of the things needed washing or mending, my grandmother would bring them home and fix them up. She was always looking for ways to make money to support the Grange.

Being the youngest, I used to go with her every Saturday morning, to take in the sights over town and help her out in the kitchen. During coffee hour she'd sell grilled English muffins, homemade muffins and hotdogs cooked in water with the rolls steamed in a colander on top; with a clean linen dish towel in it, using the lid of the kettle to hold in the steam.

Local ladies from town and a few gentlemen would come every Saturday morning for the sociability, coffee, and quite honestly gossip! The ladies as my grandmother used to say, "Think they're Ms. Astor's pet horse, all dolled up and wearing a lot of fancy clothes, and jewelry. They won't buy anything from the thrift shop; it ain't good enough for them."

The Grange had no running water and two old outhouses, so we had to lug water in jugs for coffee, and to use for cooking and dishes. One day as my grandmother was emptying a big kettle of hot water for the dishes, I was sitting on an old stool by the kitchen window, I looked up at her sweaty red face and stared at the old soiled apron she was wearing, and thought, "Poor Nana." When she put the kettle back on the stove, I jumped down and threw my arms around her belly, and laying my head on a heart that was mostly worn out, and said, "Nana don't you wish you could be like one of those ladies?" Without a second of hesitation she said, "You can't ring a hog that roots for a livin'!"

My grandmother was my heart. Although she taught me many hard lessons; and her love was often like a double edged sword. It could cut you to the core if you crossed her, and it could be just as deep and penetrating when she looked out for and comforted you. I knew at a young age, no one owed me anything, and I had two hands and I'd better learn how to use them if I expected to get by in this world.

A Little Trip over the Ossipee Mountains

When my old friend, Charlie made his first trip over the mountains, there were some two hundred natives still living there: The Welches, Pikes, Knoxes, and Eldridges. There was a little Protestant Church where ministers from different denominations preached the gospel. One Sunday a minister from Sanbornville, NH was up there doing the sermon. Three young chaps who'd been into some hard cider came in and broke up the meeting. There were plenty of good men in those mountains who would have shaped them up, and sent them home or had them arrested, but they weren't there.

Instead there happened to be a reporter who had come up from Boston to write a story. He characterized the natives as a lot of all-around bad people, when actually there was really no one in the mountains who was bad. There was only two or three people that lived over the mountain had ever been in trouble. A lot stories were started by men who went up there to work in the wintertime. Usually folks treated people as fairly as they expected to be treated. A man's word was good, and he could be trusted.

SECTION TWO

Colleen's New England Kitchen

Colleen's Pastry from

Colleen's New England Cookbook

I would like to start off with some traditional New England recipes, family recipes, and several that have been created by me. I want to say before I start this section, there isn't a hand or stand mixer on the market that beats a Kitchen-Aid Professional Hand Mixer. I've used a lot of mixers, hosted parties, cooking, and catering for over 32 years. For 15 years I serviced three large racks at a local store with homemade pastry. And the professional Stand Mixer makes homemade bread effortless.

COOKIES

I sat alone with feelings that I hadn't felt in years. I looked around at Christmas through a thick, hot blur of tears. And the candles and holly she'd arranged on every shelf...The impossibly good cookies she still somehow baked herself...A Cup of Christmas Tea

Oatmeal Cranberry White Chocolate Cookies

2/3 cup of butter or margarine, softened

¾ cup brown sugar

2 large eggs

1 ½ cups of old-fashioned oats

1 ½ cups of flour

1 teaspoon baking soda

½ teaspoon salt

1 teaspoon vanilla

1 cup dried cranberries

¾ cup white chocolate chips

Preheat oven to 350 degrees. With an electric mixer cream together the butter, sugar, eggs, vanilla, salt, oats and baking soda. Then add the 1 ½ cups of flour, mix in well. Then add cranberries and chocolate. Bake until slightly brown about 9-11 minutes.

Thinking is the hardest work there is, which is probably the reason why so few engage in it. ...Henry Ford

Colleen's Roll-Out Maple Sugar Cookies

Cream together with an electric mixer until fluffy:

1 cup of vegetable shortening

1 cup of butter

4 eggs

1/3 cup of maple syrup

2 cups of brown sugar

1 tablespoon of vanilla

2 teaspoons of maple flavoring (I use Watkins)

2 teaspoon of baking soda

½ teaspoon baking powder

Add:

6 cups of all purpose flour, 3 cups at a time

Make sure it's well blended. Put into smaller bowl, cover and refrigerate at least 1 hour. Roll out ¼ inch thick on a floured counter or pie board. Cut into desired shapes and place on cookie sheets. Bake in a 375 degree oven 7-9 minutes depending on cookie size.

You can either brush them before baking with an egg wash made with a beaten egg and ¼ cup of water, then sprinkle desired colors and decorations before baking.

Or frost with a thin vanilla or maple flavored frosting when cool, and decorate as desired.

Maple or Vanilla Frosting

3 cups of confectionary sugar

½ stick soft butter

1 teaspoon of vanilla or maple flavoring

 Add just enough evaporated milk or regular milk to make the frosting spreadable but slightly stiff.

Opportunities are usually disguised as hard work, so most people don't recognize them....Ann Landers

Nana Morrill's Hermits

Cream together:

1 cup of softened margarine

1 cup of shortening

1 ½ cups brown

1 ½ cups white sugar

½ cup molasses

4 eggs

1 teaspoon salt

1 ½ teaspoons of ginger & 1 ½ teaspoons of cinnamon

½ teaspoon of nutmeg

2 teaspoons of baking soda

ADD:

6 – 6 ½ cups of flour (2 at a time and mix real well)

Lastly:

2 cups of raisins or dates or mixture

1 cup of nut meats of your choosing

Roll out into logs on a lightly floured counter, placing one on each side of the cookie sheet. Bruch the tops with beaten egg wash and bake in a 375 degree oven 11-13 minutes. Don't overcook them.

She cried so hard she thought her bones would crack. But God mended her back together so she could still be of service to others...Colleen Bruce

Colleen's Almond Butter Cookies

1 cup of softened butter

2 cups of sugar

2 eggs

2 teaspoons of almond extract

½ teaspoon of salt

½ teaspoon of baking soda

4 ¼ cups of all purpose flour

Cream the first 6 ingredients; then add flour 1 cup at a time. Chill the mixture for about 1 hour. Then roll out ¼ inch thickness on a lightly floured surface and cut into shapes of your choosing. I brush tops with a little honey and place slivered almonds on them. Bake in 350 degree oven 8-9 minutes.

Even on the most exalted throne in the world we are only sitting on our own bottom...Michel de Montaingne

Down Home Molasses Cookies

100 year old recipe

1 cup of molasses

½ cup of sugar

2/3 cup of butter and shortening mixed

1 egg

1 tablespoon of ginger

1 tablespoon of vinegar

1 tablespoon of baking soda

2 tablespoons of cold water

4 ½ cups of all purpose flour

Mix in the order above and add flour in parts. You can refrigerate the dough and roll them thin or scoop out and press down with the bottom of a sugared glass. Bake in 350 degree oven about 12 minutes.

Well done is better than well said...Benjamin Franklin

Colleen's Peanut Butter – Honey Cookies

Cream together:

½ cup of shortening

1 cup of peanut butter

1 cup of honey

2 eggs

1 cup of sugar

1 ½ teaspoons of baking soda

1 teaspoon baking powder

½ teaspoon salt

Then add:

3 cups of flour one at a time

Roll into balls, and flatten with a fork dipped in sugar cross wise. Bake in a 350 degree oven for 8- 10 minutes.

Not enjoyment, and not in sorrow, Is our destined end or way; But to act, that each tomorrow find us further than today...Henry Wadsworth Longfellow

Colleen's Cream Cheese Christmas Cookies

Cream Together:

1 cup of soft butter

1 8 ounce package of softened cream cheese

1 ½ cups of sugar

1 egg

1 teaspoon vanilla

½ teaspoon almond extract

1 teaspoon baking powder

Add:

3 ½ cups of flour half at a time and mix well

Refrigerate dough about 1 hour then roll ¼ inch thick and cut into desired shapes. Bake in a 375 degree oven 8-10 minutes.

You can either do a light water wash before baking the add sprinkles, eyes etc. Or frost when cool. I always double the batch and frost with an almond icing.

Almond Icing

2 cups of powdered sugar

2 tablespoons of butter

½ teaspoon almond extract

Add enough cream or evaporated milk to make it the right consistency for frosting or piping.

A pessimist sees the difficulty in every opportunity; an optimist sees the opportunity in every difficulty...Sir Winston Churchill

Colleen's Chocolate chip Cookies

Cream together:

2 sticks of butter softened

1 cup of shortening

1 ½ cups of light brown sugar

1 ½ cups of white sugar

4 eggs

2 teaspoons of vanilla

1 tablespoon of instant coffee (dissolved in 2 teaspoons of warm water)

2 teaspoons of baking soda

2 teaspoons of salt

Then add one cup at a time:

5 cups of flour (the secret to good chocolate chip cookies is to blend the flour smaller amounts at a time into batter)

2 bags of chips, your choice

¾ - 1 cup chopped nuts, your choice

Bake in 375 degree oven 9-11 minutes. Do not over-bake them, as they cook more even after they are removed from the oven.

Everything that irritates us about others can lead us to an understanding of ourselves…Carl Gustav Jung

Aunt Eva's Cherry (fruit) Squares

Cream together:

2 sticks of soft margarine

2 cups of sugar

4 eggs

1 teaspoon vanilla

½ teaspoon almond extract

Add:

3 cups of flour

Spread ¾ of the batter into a greased 9x13 pan. Top with

1 can of cherry pie filling (or the flavor of your choice)

Drop in teaspoonfuls the remaining batter over the filling.

Bake in a 350 oven for 30 minutes or until a tooth pick comes out clean. Cut into squares when cool.

A little history from the 1930s actual year not known: Cream from a herd of ten cows produced $3.00 per week income. That was 14 milking(s) or 21 ½ cents per milking of 10 cows, which didn't include the chores and maintenance of the herd year round.

Apple Squares

Combines all ingredients and mix well:

1 egg

¾ cup of sugar

¼ cup of evaporated milk

1 teaspoon vanilla

¾ cup flour

1 teaspoon baking powder

½ teaspoon cinnamon

½ teaspoon salt

½ cup of chopped nuts

1 cup of chopped apple

Put into greased and floured 9x9 pan.

Sprinkle top with

1 tablespoon of sugar

½ teaspoon of cinnamon

Bake in 350 degree oven for 25 minutes. Cool and cut into bars.

Nearly all men can stand adversity, but if you want to test a man's character give him power…Abraham Lincoln

Barbara Marsh's Brownies

Mix together:

1 cup of soft butter

4 heaping tablespoons of baking cocoa

2 cups of sugar

2 teaspoons of vanilla

1 cup of flour

4 eggs

Spread into a greased and floured 9x13 pan Bake 30 minutes in a 350 degree oven. For mint brownies bake 25 minutes and cover top with a single layer of chocolate mint patties, return to oven for 5 more minutes, remove and gently spread out patties with a long spatula knife. Let cool and cut into squares.

People who know little are usually great talkers, while people who know much say little…Jean Jacques Rousseau

No Bake Cookies

In a medium kettle:

Boil exactly 3 minutes:

2 cups of sugar

2 tablespoons of cocoa (slightly rounded)

1 stick of margarine

½ cup of whole milk

Remove from stove and quickly stir in:

3 cups of quick oats

½ cup of peanut butter

1 teaspoon of vanilla

Drop by teaspoonfuls (without delay) on wax paper and let cool. Yummy!

A woman's memory from the Depression; I remember shopping for groceries in 1934 for my family. I had $6.00 every other week, and we lived well on that. I even bought strawberries one time in winter!

Colleen's Mincemeat Bars

Crumble gently with electric mixer:

2 cups of flour

1 cup of sugar

1 teaspoon baking soda

½ teaspoon salt

½ cup of oil

¼ cup of milk

Pat ¾ of the mixture into a greased 9x13 pan.

Spread over the top

3 cups of mincemeat

Cover mincemeat with remaining crumble &

¾ cup of chopped nuts.

Bake 375 degree oven for 30 minutes or until golden brown.

Cool & cut into bars.

Nothing in life is to be feared, it is only to be understood. Now is the time to understand more, so that we may fear less...Marie Curie

Old Fashioned Oatmeal Cookies

Cream Together:

¾ cup of butter, softened

1 cup of packed brown sugar

½ cup of sugar

1 egg

1 teaspoon of vanilla

3 cups of quick oats

1 ¼ teaspoons of cinnamon

½ teaspoon of baking soda

Add:

2/3 cup of flour

¾ cup of raisins (optional)

2/3 cup of chopped nuts (optional)

Drop by teaspoonfuls onto ungreased cookie sheets. Bake in 350 degree oven for 12-14 minutes.

Try not to become a man of success but rather try to become a man of value…Albert Einstein

Colleen's Butterscotch Brownies

½ cup of butter or margarine (melted)

2 cups of brown sugar

1 ½ cups of flour

2 eggs

1 teaspoon vanilla

2 teaspoon baking powder

1 ½ cups of flour

1 cup of chopped walnuts (optional)

Mix well by hand; spread into a greased 9x13 pan. Bake in a 350 degree oven for 25 minutes. Do not over-bake. Cool and cut into squares.

Not the senses I have but what I do with them is my kingdom...Helen Keller

BREADS & CAKES

Colleen's Vanilla Birthday Cake

1 cup of butter, softened

1 ½ cups of sugar

2 2/3 cups of flour

1 cup of buttermilk

4 eggs

1 tablespoon of baking powder

½ teaspoon of salt

Combined all the above ingredients and beat with an electric mixer until light and fluffy. Pour into a well greased and floured bunt pan or 9x13 cake pan. Bake in a 350 degree oven for 55 minutes. Or two round pans for 40-42 minutes.

A parent that is jealous of their child's success, is indeed a sad individual...Colleen Bruce

Colleen's Brown Bread

In a medium bowl:

Pour 1 ½ cups of boiling water **over**

1 cup of quick rolled oats

Add

2 tablespoons of shortening

2/3 cup of molasses

1 cup of corn meal

1 cup of flour

1 teaspoon baking soda

1 teaspoon of salt

Mix well with a spoon. Pour into greased container or can and steam for about 3 hours.

We never know how high we are till we are called to rise...
Emily Dickerson

Colleen's Raised Biscuits (Best Ever)

1 package of dry yeast and

2 tablespoons of sugar – dissolved in

½ cup of warm water

Let set for 5 minutes then Add:

1 cup of warm buttermilk

3 tablespoons of melted butter

4 cups of flour

2 teaspoons of baking powder

1 teaspoon of salt

Mix well until completely combined then knead on a floured counter until smooth. Cut into ½ inch thick biscuits, place on cookie sheet and cover loosely with a lint free towel. Let rise in a warm place ½ hour. Brush tops gently with evaporated milk and bake 10-12 minutes in a 400 degree oven.

1930's advertising finesse: Burma Shave signs, "You Can't Beat a Mile a Minute / But There Ain't a Future in It / or Sleep in a Chair / Nothing to Lose / but a Nap at the Wheel / Is a Permanent Snooze / Burma-Shave."

Sour Cream – Pumpkin Biscuits

Makes 2 dozen

4 cups flour

1/3 cup of sugar

1 teaspoon salt

½ teaspoon of baking soda

1 ½ cups of sour cream

1 package or 1 tablespoon of yeast

½ cup of pumpkin

1. Warm the pumpkin, sugar and sour cream to lukewarm about 80 degrees. Add the yeast and let stand for about 5 minutes. 2. Add the 3 cups of the flour, salt and baking soda. Use remaining flour to knead dough with until smooth. Place dough in a greased bowl and cover; let rise until double. Punch down and roll out on a slightly floured counter and cut into biscuits and place on cookie sheets and let rise 20 minutes. Bake in a 375 degree oven 12-15 minutes.

Time is the thing that life is made of don't squander it…Colleen Bruce

Johnny Cake

Mix well with wire whisk:

¾ cup of melted shortening

1/3 cup of sugar

2 eggs

1 cup of whole milk

1 teaspoon of salt

1 teaspoon baking soda

2 teaspoons of Baking powder

Stir In:

1 cup each of flour **and** cornmeal

Pour into a greased 8x8 pan. Bake in a 400 degree oven for 30 minutes. Serve warm with butter, maple syrup or molasses.

Good judgment comes from experience and experience – well that comes from poor judgment…Cousin Woodman

Colleen's Cheddar Cheese Bread

1 ¼ cups of milk

¾ cup of sour cream

3 tablespoons of melted butter

1 egg

1/8 teaspoon of black pepper

½ teaspoon of Italian seasoning

½ teaspoon garlic powder

1 teaspoon of salt

Whisk together really well. In a separate bowl toss together:

3 cups of flour

4-6 ounces of cheddar cheese or cheese of your choice shredded

1 tablespoon of baking powder

Stir flour mixture into liquid mixture just until combined. Don't over stir. Pour into a well greased large loaf pan. Bake in a 350 degree oven for 40-45 minutes. Let stand in pan 10 minutes before removing.

On Saturday night the young men on the farm would pile into the Ford, and go to the dance hall in town. This was their

reward for having done two weeks work in one...Colleen Bruce

Colleen's Old Fashioned Donuts

Blend well with an electric mixer:

1 ½ tablespoons of butter melted

1 ½ cups of sugar

2 eggs

1 cup applesauce

½ teaspoon salt

½ teaspoon baking soda

½ teaspoon **each** of nutmeg and cinnamon

4 teaspoons of baking powder

Gently Blend in with mixer:

4 cups of flour

On a floured counter roll out dough, and cut with a donut cutter. OR thin the batter down with 2/3 cup of whole milk and put into donut batter drop Maker (NORPRO Brand)

Fry in hot grease (I use vegetable shortening) 375 degrees for 3-5 minutes, turning over part way through.

1930's school days. School boys were lucky to have one pair of overalls. Mom would wash them out at night, so they'd always be clean for the next day. The warming ovens were used for drying something every night.

My uncle shook out his pipe one more time, and guided by the light in the kitchen window he walked home across the pasture. Only stopping briefly to look up at the cold winter sky and taking in one more deep breath...Colleen Bruce

Maple Oatmeal Bread

Makes 2 Loaves

In a large bowl pour:

2 cups of boiling water over -

2 cups rolled oats

Add

1 tablespoon butter

½ cup of maple syrup

1 teaspoon salt

In a measuring cup dissolve

2 packages or 2 tablespoons of dry yeast

½ teaspoon sugar

2/3 cup lukewarm water

Add dissolved yeast to the oatmeal mixture

5 cups of flour

Mix in about 4 cups of flour

Knead in the remainder of the flour. Knead about 10 minutes

Place dough in a greased bowl, cover and let rise in a warm place until doubled in size. Punch down, put on a floured counter and divide into 2 loaves. Place in two greased bread pans, let rise again. Preheat oven to 375 degrees and bake for 40 minutes until brown.

We can build walls or we can build bridges, either way we're going to build something...Colleen Bruce

Corn Muffins

Whisk together:

1 1/13 cups of sugar

1 teaspoon of salt

1 can of cream style corn (regular size)

11/2 cups of cornmeal

½ cup of oil

4 large eggs

1 cup of milk

2 tablespoons of baking powder

Stir in by hand just until blended:

3 ¼ cups of flour

Preheat oven to 375 degrees. Scoop batter into cup cake paper lined or greased muffin tins, makes 12 large or 16 smaller muffins. Bake 15 – 20 minutes, test centers with tooth pick.

Happiness is inward, and not outward; and so, it does not depend on what we have, but on what we are…Henry Van Dyke

Kim's Carrot Cake

2 cups of sugar

3 large eggs

2 cups flour

1 teaspoon **each** of ginger and cinnamon

½ teaspoon of salt

3 cups of carrots shredded

1 cup of **corn oil** (this is a must)

2 teaspoons of vanilla

¾ cup of crushed pineapple

1 cup of coconut

1 cup of chopped nuts (optional)

Mix all ingredients well with electric mixer.

Pour into large round, spring-form or 9x13 pan greased well and FLOURED.

Bake in 350 degree oven for about 1 hour, test center with toothpick.

COLLEEN'S CREAM CHEESE FROSTING

1 8 ounce package of softened cream cheese

½ stick of butter softened

3 cups of confectionery sugar

1 teaspoon vanilla extract

Just enough evaporated milk, or half and half (2-4 tablespoons) to make the frosting spreadable.

She cooked for the love of giving to others, instead of cooking until she was all worn-out from trying to make a living...Colleen Bruce

Aunt Goldie's Fruit Cake

Cream together:

1 cup of sugar

½ cup of shortening

1 egg

1 teaspoon of vanilla,

1 teaspoon of almond

1 teaspoon of lemon flavoring

ADD:

1 cup of hot black coffee

½ teaspoon **each** of baking soda & salt

1 1/3 cups of flour

In a separate bowl toss:

½ cup **each** of dates, raisins, mixed dried fruit (or dried cherries/pineapple) chopped nuts in

1/3 cup of flour

Stir into batter and pour into a well greased and floured bunt pan. Bake in a 325 degree oven for 60-75 minutes, half way through place cherries and pecan halves around the top.

1930s a time all should have experienced. Fathers would put tire patches on the sides or tops of the children's shoes, and boots to keep the water and snow out. To polish the boots and shoes, they used tallow, a by-product from butchering. This would not only polish them beautifully but would water-proof them.

PIES & OTHER SWEET TREATS

My Daughter Jessie, 3 Years Old - Making Pies.

Colleen's Pie Crust

In a stainless steel bowl put:

4 cups of all purpose flour

1 ¾ cups of solid vegetable shortening

2 teaspoons of salt

1 teaspoon of sugar

½ teaspoon of baking powder

Crumble this with an electric mixer (I have found with ALL my cooking and baking, you can't beat for any amount of money a KITCHEN-AID MIXER) on medium speed moving rather quickly. You want crumble not a clump.

Add gingerly:

¾ - 1 cup of cold tap water (as cold as it will run)

You want your dough to leave the sides of the bowl and form a soft pliable ball. I always tell people when I teach them to make pies. Handle your crust like a newborn baby gently; but handle it with confidence like you know what you're doing. Don't overwork it and use the flour on your counter or board sparingly. When you roll it use only light pressure, not like your crushing nuts with a rolling pin!

And always use a flat wide spatula knife to gently release the dough from the counter so your edges won't tear. This recipe makes one 2 crust pie and one shell.

Slower than cold molasses running uphill on a frosty morning...Nana Morrill

Old Fashioned New England Mincemeat

In a Big Kettle put:

½ Bushel of Cortland or Macintosh Apples, peeled and cored, stewed these first like applesauce in the kettle. Cover the apples with a pot of hot coffee (see below) add water as needed.

Add:

3 pounds of cooked, finely ground venison or beef (less expensive cuts of beef, venison tougher cuts)

1 12-cup pot of strong black coffee

1 ½ cups of molasses

4 cups of dark brown sugar

1 stick of butter

1 teaspoon of nutmeg

1 teaspoon of salt

½ teaspoon of cloves

2 tablespoons of cinnamon

1 regular sized box of golden raisins

1 regular sized box of regular raisins

Cook on a low simmer for at least 4-6 hours.

Can in quart jars in a hot water bath for 45 minutes. Or freeze in containers of your choosing. I often make one to eat right away and freeze some pies frozen unbaked for a later time or to sell.

Some folks know it's part of their duty in life to make sure others get a square deal...Colleen Bruce

Colleen's Apple Pie Filling

This is a creation of mine, and has pleased everyone who's ever eaten it!

In a medium mixing bowl – mix the following ingredient with a spoon:

5-6 cups of sliced apples (depending on the size of your pie plate)

I mix the apples usually – Macs or Cortlands with Jonagolds or Granny Smith.

½ cup of light brown sugar

¾ - 1 cup of white sugar

2 teaspoons of strawberry jello

1 tablespoon of flour

½ teaspoon cinnamon

¼ teaspoon nutmeg

1 teaspoon of vanilla

½ stick of butter melted

Make the pie crust recipe above. (I always grease my pie plate) Dust the top of the bottom crust with about 2 teaspoons of flour, pour filling mixture in and gently pat it down. Place top crust on, seal the edges and brush the top with evaporated milk. Bake in a 350 degree oven about 1 hour or until golden brown.

"And remember, apple pie without the cheese is like a kiss without the squeeze!"

I'd rather pay their board then feed em'...Nana Morrill

Colleen's Indian Pudding

In a medium bowl, microwave, stirring halfway through with a wire whisk cook until thick:

2 ¾ cups of water

½ stick of butter

½ teaspoon salt

1 cup of yellow cornmeal

Then add and mix with electric mixer, until smooth:

1 teaspoon of cinnamon

1 teaspoon of nutmeg

½ teaspoon ginger

2 ¼ cups of whole milk (I use 12 ounce can of evaporated milk as part of this, it makes for a richer pudding)

6 large eggs

1 cup of molasses

2/3 cup brown sugar

1 teaspoon of vanilla

Pour into buttered casserole dish and set in a larger cake pan with water at least half way up the sides of the dish. Bake in a 350 degree oven 60-75 minutes or until a tooth pick comes out clean. Remove from pan and cool on wire rack, serve warm with vanilla ice cream or whipped cream.

He said he wasn't hungry, but this is what he ate...Nana Morrill

Colleen's Grape-Nut Custard Pudding

Butter or spray a 2 quart casserole dish. Then spread evenly on the bottom:

1 ¼ Post grapenuts cereal

1 12 ounce can of evaporated milk (pour over the cereal and let soak at least ½ hour.)

In a separate bowl mix with electric mixer:

4 cups of whole milk

6 large eggs

2 teaspoons of vanilla

1 ¼ cups of sugar

Pinch of salt

Pour over cereal mixture and stir gently with a spoon. Set in a pan filled with enough water to come half way up the sides of the dish. Bake in a 350 degree oven about 60-75 minutes. Until a tooth pick comes out clean. Serve warm or cold.

Trust people to be who they are, believe them when they tell you, and you won't get disappointed...Colleen Bruce

Nana Morrill's Popcorn Balls

Have popped and ready in a large bowl:

10 cups of plain popped popcorn

In a sauce pan put:

1 cup of molasses

1 cup of corn syrup

3 tablespoons of butter

1 tablespoon of vinegar

Boil to a hard ball stage about 250 degrees. Pour over popcorn; stir quickly with a large fork. Butter your hands with soft butter, scoop up about 1 cup at a time and press and shape into balls, place on wax paper and keep repeating.

Stay in your own lane and let God work on your life. It will not only save you a lot of heartache but it will bless you as well...Michelle Duff

Colleen's Easy Peanut Butter Fudge

In a medium pan bring to a boil and cook **exactly** 3 minutes:

2 cups of white sugar

½ cup of whole milk

Just before removing

Add:

2 cups mini marshmallows

Remove from stove and quickly stir in:

1 cup of peanut butter

Put into a wax paper lined 9x9 pan and cool at room temperature. Cut into squares.

The winds of change blow through our life, sometimes gently, sometimes like a tropical storm...The Language of Letting Go

Nana's Coffee Jello

Dissolve:

2 envelopes of plain Knox gelatin in

½ cup of hot water

Add:

½ white sugar

3 cups of plain cold strong coffee

Refrigerate and let set up, serve with whip cream or evaporated milk and a little sugar sprinkled on top.

A favorite patriotic Great Depression motto: Eat it Up, Wear it Out, Make It Do, Or Do Without...

CANNING DELIGHTS

Nana Morrill's Piccalilli

In a roaster oven liner or other x-large kettle put:

7 pounds EACH of red & green tomatoes chopped up

6 red AND 6 green peppers cut up small

12 medium-large onions cut up small

Cover with 1 cup of canning salt (table salt) and let stand 4 hours. Drain off liquid and then add:

4 pounds of brown sugar

1 teaspoon of whole cloves

1 tablespoon of mustard seed

1 heaping tablespoon of cinnamon

3 cups of cider vinegar

Cook at a low boil for about 20 minutes. I like mine a little firmer rather than soft.

Meanwhile have hot clean jars and lids ready to pack. Process filled jars making sure rims are clean before putting tops on, for 15 minutes in boiling hot water bath.

If you have to tear someone else down to feel better, you'll be sick your whole life...Colleen Bruce

Nana Morrill's Bread & Butter Pickles

In an x-large kettle cover the following with 1/3 cup of salt:

32 cups of medium – thin sliced cucumbers (NOT peeled)

6 medium onions sliced into thin strips

2 cloves chopped or 1 rounded tablespoon of jarred garlic

Cover top with about 8 cups of ice cubes. Let stand at least 2 hours, drain off liquid and remove any small ice pieces. Put kettle on stove and add:

7 cups of white sugar

1 ½ teaspoons of turmeric

1 ½ teaspoons of celery seed

2 tablespoons of mustard seed

2 ½ cups of cider vinegar

Bring to a boil slowly and simmer about 5 minutes. Process in clean hot jars, place in a water bath about 15-20 minutes.

The Great Depression brought out the best in people. When there was no money, trading took the place of cash. Clothing alterations were often traded for babysitting, or wall papering a room for someone, who could spare some ham, was considered a good trade.

Greta's Maple Bread & Butter Pickles

40 cups of medium – thin sliced cucumbers (NOT peeled)

9 large sliced onion

4 large green peppers cut small

2/3 cup of salt

Drain and Add:

4 cups of dark maple syrup

7 cups of white sugar

3 teaspoons EACH of celery seed & turmeric

4 tablespoons of mustard seed

4 cups of vinegar

FOLLOW SAME STEPS FOR PROCESSING

AS ABOVE

We are sturdy beings. But in many ways, we are fragile. We can accept change and loss, but this comes at our own pace and timing in our own way. And only we and God can determine the timing...Codependent No More

Bev's Carrot Cake Jam

This is beyond good!

Simmer for 20 minutes covered, stirring frequently:

2 cups of finely shredded carrots (4 medium)

1 15-ounce can of crushed pineapple

1 cup of finely chopped pears (I use 2 snack sized cups)

2 tablespoons of lemon juice

Remove from heat and add:

1 13/4 ounce package of powdered pectin

Bring to a boil for 1 minute then add:

1 teaspoon of cinnamon

½ teaspoon of nutmeg

4 cups of white sugar

2 cups of brown sugar

¼ cup of coconut

¼ cup of raisins (optional)

1 teaspoon of vanilla

Return to heat and boil for 1 minute. Then quickly fill hot jars with hot rims and lids. Process in boiling water 10 minutes

This above all: to thine own self be true, and it must follow, as the night the day, thou'canst not then be false to any man...William Shakespeare

HEARTIER FARE & OTHER DELITES

Colleen's New England Boiled-Dinner

1 3-4 pound smoked ham shoulder or corned-beef brisket

1 small medium sized head of cabbage, quartered, but not cored

10 medium carrots peeled

10 potatoes peeled or unpeeled and washed

1 heaping tablespoon of pickling spice

3 bay leaves

1 rounded tablespoon of jarred minced or chopped garlic

In a very large crock pot or a large heavy gage kettle on the stove top, put corned beef first, then spices, then carrots, then potatoes and last on the very top the quartered cabbage. Cover with water at least ¾ of the way over everything in the pot. Bring to a boil and then on a low, but steady simmering boil cook for about 4 hours in crock pot on high, and about 3 hours on a low boil on the stove top.

Beets do separately or used canned

1 medium turnip

Peeled, diced and boiled until fork tender in plenty of water with 1 teaspoon of sugar in the water. Cook separately, drain and then mash and add:

1 stick of butter

¼ cup brown sugar

½ teaspoon salt

¼ teaspoon black pepper

When winter winds are piercing chill, And through the hawthorn blows the gale, With solemn feet I tread the hill that over brows the lonely vale…Henry Wadsworth Longfellow

Colleen's Fish Chowder

Four servings:

1 ½ - 2 pounds firm white fish, such as haddock or cod

¼ cup diced salt pork or smoked bacon, diced

1 medium onion, diced

3 medium potatoes in 1inch cubes

2 ½ cups water (Cook all the above on a low simmer until completely cooked)

1 12-ounce can of evaporated milk

1 cup of heavy cream or whole milk or combination of the two

4 tablespoons butter

Kosher or sea salt and freshly ground pepper to taste

Chopped fresh flat leaf parsley, thyme or chives for garnish, optional

Heat a heavy pot over medium heat and add bacon or salt pork. Cook until lightly browned, add onion and butter and cook, stirring, until onion is translucent. Add water, potatoes and thyme and cook until potatoes are nearly done. Add the fish. Cook until it's opaque. Add evaporated milk, cream or milk or a mixture of the two. Simmer 8-10 minutes. Remove the pot from the heat, taste broth and add salt and pepper to taste. The flavor of chowder improves if it rests for 30 minutes or more and can it be reheated over low heat but not boiled.

Rosicky would put on his cap and jacket and slip down to the barn and give his work-horses a little extra oat, letting them eat out of his hand in their slobbery fashion. It was his way of expressing how he felt, and made him chuckle with pleasure...Neighbor Rosicky

Grammy Grant's Poor Man's Soup

In a medium kettle fry:

¼ pound of bacon or salt pork until crisp

Add:

4-6 potatoes diced up small

2 onions cut up small

Cover with water about 1 inch over the top and boil until potatoes are done.

Add:

1 can of evaporated milk

1-11/2 cups of whole milk

Salt and pepper to taste

It is better to build strong children than to repair broken men...Fredrick Douglas

Colleen's Hamburg Soup

In a medium sized kettle scramble

2 pounds of hamburger (using just enough water so it won't stick to the bottom of the kettle while cooking)

Add:

5 medium potatoes cut up small

2 medium onions cut up small

3 carrots cut into small slices

3 stalks of celery cut into small slices

8-10 cups of water or more if needed

6-7 beef bouillon cubes

3 tablespoons of gravy master

1 tablespoon of jarred garlic, optional

2 bay leaves

1 teaspoon of poultry seasoning

¼ teaspoon black pepper

Cook on a low simmer – boil until vegetables are done. Then add 1 cup of uncooked pasta shells or elbow macaroni and simmer another 15-20 minutes.

Hospitality is more than the food we make, it's being prepared to open our hearts to our visitors and make them truly feel welcome…Colleen Bruce

Colleen's Crock Pot Mac and Cheese

Spray the inside of your crock pot with or without a liner, with cooking spray. Then add all at once:

1 pound of uncooked macaroni, your choice

1 pound of cubed up brick cheese, your choice

1 stick of butter

6 cups of whole milk

1 teaspoon salt

½ teaspoon of black pepper

1 small onion grated, optional

Cook on high for about one and a half hours, stir gently and cook on high 1 more hour or on low another 2 hours depending on when you need it. It's yummy and easy.

Do not neglect to show hospitality to strangers, for by this some have entertained angels without knowing it. (Hebrews 13:2)

Colleen's Pork Pie Filling

Cook in about **1 ½ cups of water** in a good sized kettle chopping it up small as you go along:

1 ½ pounds of plain ground pork

1 pound of hamburger

1 large onion finely chopped

2 teaspoons of salt

½ teaspoon of black pepper

1/4 teaspoon of allspice

1 tablespoon of cinnamon

1 tablespoon of poultry seasoning

In a separate kettle cook:

6 large potatoes (I like Yukon Gold)

Mash them with:

½ stick of butter

1 Cup of sour cream,

Add:

potato mixture to the cooked meat and blend well. Make 3 good sized pork pies. Use bottom and top crust, brush top with milk and bake in 350 degree oven about 1 hour or until golden brown. They can be frozen unbaked.

During the Depression everything was patched or darned. When collars or cuffs wore out, Mother or Grandmother turned them inside out and sewed them back on. Or knitted or sewed an extension on sleeves and pant legs.

Colleen's Turkey / Chicken Pie Filling

In a good sized kettle, make gravy first:

3 cups of stock

1 12 ounce can of evaporated milk

3 cups of whole milk

1 stick of butter

4-5 chicken or turkey base or bullion cubes

1 tablespoon of gravy master

4 slightly rounded tablespoons of flour or 3 of corn starch

½ teaspoon of black pepper

Bring all these ingredients to a low boil stir frequently with a wire whisk. Be sure to not let it catch on the bottom of the kettle. **Then Add:**

5-6 cups of cut up turkey or chicken

If you have left over stuffing you can add some of that too. Some people like to add some canned or frozen veggie, which is fine. Our family makes it plain and has vegetables as a side. You can make this into two crust pies about (2 large) or cover while hot with homemade biscuits or use Bisquick according to the box, and bake until biscuits are golden brown and not doughy on the bottom. Pies bake in 350 degree oven 1 hour or until golden brown. Pies or biscuits brush the tops with evaporated milk.

For generations this has been our traditional family stuffing recipe.

Homemade New England Cracker Stuffing

1 small-medium onion

2 stalks of celery

Sauté in 1 stick of butter until tender

4 sleeves (1 pound box) saltine crackers crushed

3 eggs

1 teaspoon salt

½ teaspoon of pepper

1 tablespoon poultry seasoning (I like Bells)

3-3 1/2 cups of whole milk

You can either stuff a bird just before baking or bake in a buttered casserole dish until cooked in the middle and lightly brown in a 350 degree oven for about 1 hour.

For whom the Lord loves He reproves, even as a father corrects his son in whom he delights. (Proverbs 3:12)

Aunt Colleen's Roast Pork or Lamb

3-4 pound piece of meat (usually bone-in)

Take two long sheet of aluminum foil and fold tight straight creases back and forth a couple of time to insure a good sealed seam. Spray generously with cooking spray and sprinkle evenly on the foil:

1/3 cup of flour

2 heaping tablespoons of jarred minced garlic

1 tablespoon of poultry seasoning

1 teaspoon of salt

½ teaspoon of black pepper

Roll the meat firmly but without tearing the foil, until completely covered with this mixture. Make a loose tent over the top of the meat and sealing the sides, but not too snugly.

Bake in a 350 oven on a rack over a pan of water for about 3 1/2 hours. Make sure the pan has water in it. The meat will be crusty on the top, juicy in the middle and you'll have a lot of drippings to make gravy. I also cook my venison roast the same way.

Serve with mint jelly, mashed potato or baked potato with sour cream, spinach and warm applesauce!

We cannot grow spiritually without developing a prayer life. Time with God is essential to hearing His voice even in the midst of noise and turmoil...Colleen Bruce

New England Baked Beans

A traditional New England staple every Saturday night!

Regardless of the type of beans you are making, soak them covered with cold water at least 16-24 hours before cooking.

1 pound of Red kidney, Jacob's cattle or Soldier Beans

Drain the beans you've soaked and cover with fresh water, parboil at least 20 minutes or until you blow on them and the skins split.

1 medium to large onion cut up small

1/3 cup of regular or spicy brown mustard

½ teaspoon of black pepper

2 teaspoons of salt

1 ¼ cups of brown sugar

½ or more cut up salt pork or bacon

Use the water you parboiled them in to cover by at least 3 inches.

In the oven cook in a bean pot making sure they stay covered with water, (adding 1-2 cups every hour or so) for about 6-7 hours in a 350 degree oven or in a crock pot on low about 6-7 hours, on high about 5 hours.

1 pound of Pea Beans or Pinto Beans

1 medium to large onion cut up small

1 cup of molasses

¼ cup of brown sugar

2 tablespoons of mustard (your choice)

¼ teaspoon of black pepper

2 teaspoons of salt

½ cup of cut up salt pork or bacon

Follow the direction above.

Under the spreading chestnut-tree the village smithy stands; The smith, a mighty man is he, with large and sinewy hands; and the muscles of his arms are strong as iron bands...Henry Wadsworth Longfellow

Colleen's Stuffed Eggs

1 dozen hard boiled eggs (Bring eggs covered with water to a complete boil, remove from burner with the cover on

and let sit15 minutes in hot water. They'll be cooked perfectly)

Take peeled eggs cut in half and remove yolks to a small bowl and add:

1 regular sized can of deviled ham

1 tablespoon of spicy brown mustard

¼ teaspoon each of salt

¼ teaspoon of black pepper

1 cup of miracle whip or mayonnaise

Fill empty white halves and arrange on platter. I often lightly sprinkle tops with paprika. Refrigerate until you're ready to serve.

It is the blessings of the Lord that makes rich, and it adds no sorrow to it. (Proverbs 10:22)

Butternut or Blue Hubbard Squash

New England Style

1 large or 2 small butternut squash or 1 blue Hubbard peeled and seeds removed

Cook until fork tender, remove from stove, drain and mash. Then add:

½ - 1 stick of butter

1 teaspoon salt

¼ teaspoon black pepper

½ cup of brown sugar

In the Great Depression gift wrap was removed with the utmost care, so that it could be carefully smoothed and put away in a draw for another use.

To Corn Your Own Beef by Colleen

In a large bean pot or crock combine and stir well:

8 cups of warm tap water

2/3 cup of salt

3 tablespoons of brown sugar

2 bay leaves

1 minced clove of garlic or heaping tablespoon of jarred

2 teaspoons of pickling spice

2 teaspoons of mustard seed

1 tablespoon of peppercorns

1 large cinnamon stick broke in half

2 tablespoons of cider vinegar

Put your meat in and swirl it around well. Refrigerate and in 2 days turn it over, on the fourth or fifth day remove the meat, don't rinse it. Cook in a crock pot covered with water on low until fork tender. Put vegetables on top: carrots, potatoes and cabbage last. Cook for about 4 hours on low once it starts to boil.

THE OPEN WINDOW

The old house by the lindens
Stood silent in the shade,
And on the graveled pathway
The light and shadow played.

I saw the nursery windows
Wide open to the air;
But the faces of the children,
They were no longer there.

The large Newfoundland house-dog
Was standing by the door;
He looked for his playmates,
Who would return no more.

They walked not under lindens,
They played not in the hall;
But shadow, and silence, and sadness
Were hanging over all.

The birds sang in the branches,
With sweet, familiar tone;
But voices of the children

Will be heard in dreams alone!

And the boy that walked beside me,
He could not understand
Why closer in mine, ah! Closer,
I pressed his warm, soft hand!

...Henry Wadsworth Longfellow

Baby Morgan

Homemade Baby Formula

Mix:

12 ounce can of evaporated milk

18 ounces of boiled water

2 tablespoons of Karo syrup

Place in sterilized bottle and refrigerate up to 2 days.

MEASUREMENTS

- a pinch....................1/8 teaspoon or less
- 3 teaspoons...............1 tablespoon
- 4 tablespoons.............1/4 cup
- 8 tablespoons.............1/2 cup
- 12 tablespoons............3/4 cup
- 16 tablespoons............1 cup
- 2 cups......................1 pint
- 4 cups......................1 quart
- 4 quarts.................1 gallon
- 8 quarts.................1 peck
- 4 pecks..................1 bushel
- 16 ounces...............1 pound
- 32 ounces...............1 quart
- 1 ounce liquid..........2 tablespoons
- 8 ounces liquid.........1 cup

NANA MORRILL'S SAYINGS and

OTHER IDIOMS

- "If you bought him / her for what they know and sold them for what they think they know, you'd be a millionaire!"
- When it came to smoking my great grandfather used to say, "A little fire to one end and a little fool to the other."
- When it came to drinking my grandmother used to say, "It's not the last drink that gets you intoxicated, it's the first one."
- "They're smart where the skin is off."
- "They picked a real lemon in the garden of love where they say only peaches grow."
- A real penny pincher: "He's so cheap he'd skin anything to save a nickel, and ruin a ten cent jackknife!"
- Living beyond your means: "There's someone with a champagne appetite and a beer man's pocketbook."
- "Slower than cold molasses running up hill on a frosty morning."
- "He knows too much for one man, but not enough for two."
- "By the time I get done with them, they'll wish they hadn't seen me today!"

- "By the time I can get an appointment with the doctor, I can see the undertaker; and I don't need an appointment with him."
- "They lived here about 80 years; too bad they never did become a native."
- "A man or woman is only as good as their word. If their word's no good then they ain't much better."
- A personal debt that never seems to get paid, "I'd rather owe you than cheat you out of it."
- How to avoid death and illness, "They can't hit a moving target!"
- Your ability to do something, "I can shoot straight if I don't have to shoot far."
- When someone overcharges you or cheats you out of money: "If I bought them for that, then I bought them pretty cheap!"
- "The quickest way to a man's heart is through his stomach."
- "Lovin' don't last, but cookin' do!"
- My grandmother used to holler this up the stairs every school morning: "Rally around the rag boys, rally once again."
- "If they were no good when they were living, they aren't no better now they're dead."
- "We'd better get going we're burning daylight."
- "Pretty is as pretty does."

- When you're at a stop sign and it's clear to go: "Take it away Rosedale."
- When you're ready to go home and can't wait to get there; "Home James, and don't spare the horses!"
- When the odds are stacked pretty high against something turning out right: "It's like trying to make a silk purse out of a sow's ear."
- My grandmother used to be able to take little or nothing and make a meal fit for a king."
- When someone swears a lot: "That's pretty rough language you're using."
- Not knowing what you're getting yourself into spending money. "A fool and his money are soon parted."
- "You've got two hands and you'd better learn how to use them, because no one owes you a thing."
- "They pulled into the door-yard." That's a driveway around here.
- "You'll get a licking if you don't straighten out!" That's a spanking for a child.
- "Let's go cungen around." That's a word that means looking for something that you can't find easily.
- When someone has something and they don't offer to share it with those around them. "What are they like dead men, one in a box?"
- 'I can shoot straight if I don't have to shoot far."

- "One bad apple in the bunch can ruin the whole barrel." That's what one trouble maker can do in a group.
- "You're as good as the company you keep."
- My grandmother used to say about the kids we would hang out with, especially if they got into trouble. "Just because someone else go to the bathroom in the brook and drinks the water below, that's no sight that you have too!"
- "They lie so much they believe it."
- "They lie just like a rug."
- If you see or hear about something or when it comes to food that you're not sure of. "I ain't ever had it and I don't want it again."
- When my grandmother was mad she'd say; "I'll run up one side of them and down the other and they'll know somebody's had a hold of them!"
- When you need to make big changes or put your foot down with someone, but there's no need to eliminate them. "Don't through the baby out with the bath water."
- "Get... While the getting is good." Means you better get moving or get out of a situation before it's too late.
- When someone is really nervous. "They're more nervous than a cat trying to cover up litter on a hot tin roof!"
- When another location isn't too far away. "Just down the road a piece."

- The distance that's hard to explain. "By the way a crow flies it's over there."
- "It's not the dead you have to fear, it's the living that'll hurt you."
- Put on your big boy / big girl pants, you're shaving now.
- If you're bored then you must not have any dirty curtains, windows and wall.
- "I can't never did anything."
- They're like the thief that went to jail. They're not sorry they stole, but they're awful sorry they got caught!
- Go ahead and quit then they've beaten you twice.
- If you work like a horse then you eat like one.
- "Don't get your water hot!" What you say when you can see someone is getting mad.
- "Don't get on the wrong side of them." This is a warning about someone who has a bad temper.
- "I'll lay them out in lavender!" This is telling someone off in a way they'll understand. Or, "When I get done with them, they'll know somebody's had them."
- "They're smart where the skin is off." Comparing a persons' understanding about something, to how it feels when you scrape your knees or the palm of your hands and it tears the skin off.
- Sometimes it takes a bigger man to just walk away.

- "Give em' the whole nine yards!" Means give all you got.
- "I'm as tired as I ever want to be." Means you're very tired from a lot of work and perhaps even life.
- When you're tired, and it's getting late, and want your company to go home. "Make yourselves at home I am, and wish you were."
- "It's not all it / they are cracked up to be." Means someone or something isn't what it appears.
- "It's a lot easier to let the cat out of the bag then it is to put him back in!"
- "There's three people in their world; me, myself and I," This is a sure sign of a selfish person.

I want to end this section with a couple of poems, and short rhymes my Nana Morrill taught me between the ages of five and twelve years old. It's still a comfort to me to recall them to my mind.

The American Flag

Don't tell people what this is about; see if they can guess at the end.

When freedom from her mountain height
Unfurled her standard to the air
She tore her azure robe of night
And set the stars of glory there.
She mingled with its gorgeous dyes
The milky baldric of the skies,
And striped its pure celestial white
With streaking of the morning light,
Then from his mansion in the sun
She called her eagle bearer down
And gave into his mighty hand
The symbol of the chosen land…
The American Flag by Joseph Rodman Drake

When I was a Little Girl

I was little girl (boy) about so high,

Mumma took a little stick and made me

cry, Now I'm a big girl (boy)Mumma can't

do Daddy takes a big stick and goes right

to!

I Love Coffee – I Love Tea

I love coffee, I love tea,

I love the boys and the boys love me.

 I wish my Ma would hold her tongue,

because she had a fellow when she was

young.

I wish my Pa would do the same, because

he's the one that changed her name.

SECTION THREE

FOOD FOR THOUGHT

My Three Older Siblings and I (1966)

Insight and Inspiration

When I started this section of the book, I prayed about how to present it. What I do know was it had to be written in such a way that I would leave those reading it inspired and comforted for having done so. It's pertinent to mention that the first three decades of my life were less than desirable, overshadowed with domestic, societal and generational abuse, addiction, trauma, and loss.

However, with a hard - won journey through recovery work and healing; with a more – often - than not struggling relationship with God, the Father through Jesus Christ I have been able to do more than survive; I've been able to thrive. The following short stories and poems are part of what has been thought provoking and has contributed to my personal growth.

The details may vary, but heart pain is heart pain. Loss is loss and hope will always beget hope. Love needs to be loved. More importantly, "The truth, just like God, is independent and stands alone, and they will never need anyone or anything, because they just are.

- *Behold, children are a gift of the Lord. The fruit of the womb is a reward. (psalm 127:3)*

- *Grandchildren are the crown of old men, And the glory of sons is their fathers. (Proverbs 17:6)*

- *Your eyes have seen my unformed substance; And in your book all written the days that were ordained for me; When as yet there was not one of them. (Psalm 139:16)*

- *But Jesus said, "Let the children alone, and do not hinder them from coming to Me; for the kingdom of heaven belongs to such as these." (Matthew 19:14)*

- *Fathers, do not provoke your children to anger, but bring them up in the discipline and instruction of the Lord. (Ephesians 6:4)*

- *For I am confident of this very thing, that he who began a good work in you will perfect it until the day of Christ Jesus. (Philippians 1:6)*
- *I have no greater joy than this, to hear of my children walking in truth. (3 John 1:4)*

This particular piece is a personal view and interpretation from life experiences that I have had. And in all its complexity has been and is near and dear to my heart.

Children Are Not Rubber-Bands

By Colleen Bruce

Have you ever met an adult to including yourself, or a teenager, that doesn't have stories about their childhood? For example how they lived, what they ate, how they were treated. Family traditions and other things leave the greatest impression upon them. I believe all of us can boast of these things, in both good and bad ways. I remember in the early stages of my counseling and recovery, my mind swirling around with disbelief as I unpacked my childhood and school years. Often I would leave my counselor's office and think on the drive home, "How is it possible that I'm not in a psychiatric hospital?"

As parents, caregivers, teachers, doctors, and other adult professionals, and even as peers; we believe we have the formula down pat with the right answers and solutions for a child's or teenager's life. We want to believe that we're beyond the things that happened to us in our formative years.

If this were true and children are as resilient as adults like to deceive themselves into believing, then why are there so many emotionally, spiritually, and physically troubled adults?

Here's where the rubber hits the road for me. When a children have a broken bones, severe cold, or the flu, scraped knees or bruises; they have the bounce of a rubber ball. One minute they're fighting a 103 temperature and vomiting; the next minute they're outside playing in the dirt. An adult with these symptoms would be 3 days getting back to normal. In my humble opinion that's where a child's resiliency ends.

I am not a doctor and I don't pretend to play one on TV, but I have a lot of childhood experiences starting with rejection in the womb. I experienced the traumatic loss of both my parents before, the age of three; multi-generational caregivers that passed on verbal, physical, emotional, and sexual abuse; as well as addiction. For over two decades I had family, teachers, and other professionals ostracize me. My peers did the same and bullied me as well. The answer was to start medicating me with Donnatal Elixir at five years old; to cope with life and to help me stop crying relentlessly. Some of you might ask, "Why would a child made of resiliency need medication to survive?"

Today, I have answers for my own life and better insight into parenting than I had when my children were in their formative years. It would be reckless and unwise, to say the least, for me to try and inform another human being about child rearing without letters after my name.

However, I serve a great God, who is my Heavenly Father. With His guidance and much prayerful insight, I feel confident to offer a list of questions that might enlighten not only you, but also those around you. I am a staunch believer that what we learn, how we are treated and taught in our formative years and who our caregivers are, have the greatest impact on our teenage and adults years, as well as our perception of God. Ask yourself these questions for the children in your life and then ask them for yourself. Ponder them if you see any of these things happening.

If Children are Resilient Then

- Why are there so many children, teens and adults taking medication, sitting in the counselor's office, or being kicked out of school?
- Why are they acting out: stealing, lying, sneaking, and hiding food, toys and other items?
- Why are they self mutilating; biting nails, digging at their skin and making marks, pulling their hair out, and having nightmares?
- Why are they sneaking cigarettes, alcohol, drugs, and other mind altering substances?
- Why are they wetting the bed, having bowel movements in their pants or not wanting to take a bath or be touched?

- Why are they eating until they are sick to their stomach or not being able to have any restraint from salty or sugary foods and candy?

- Why are the crying almost relentlessly, and getting hysterical, and acting out over what appears to be the littlest things or with - drawing to the point of refusing to answer?

- Why are they having separation anxiety (more often than not from the abuser and can't be calmed down and crying to the point of hyperventilation?

- Why are they running away from home, becomes aggressive towards the adults in their lives, or becoming a school or cyber bullies?

- Why do they starting to have sexual relationships before the age of 13 or having an obvious inappropriate interest in sexual things?

- Why are so many children, turned adult (parents, and professionals) so angry, resentful, controlling, untrusting, or abusive?

- What makes you or the people you know act, think, believe and live the way you do?

- What causes children or adults to trigger? What gets to their core in a flash without any warning and why?

- How do you believe you are doing as a parent, spouse, friend, sibling or professional? Are you making the grade, cutting the mustard?

- Last, but most importantly: why do we have children? Do they have to be here? Do they have any say in their arrival? Is it the "fashionable thing to do," or just part of what has become known as "normal" to have a baby and start a family? Are they brought here as a means of income or support for the adults who have them, or are they born out love, and want of a family?

Final thought, as sobering as these questions and thoughts are it would behoove every human being to do a little soul searching in terms of a child and their life. Most people have a choice, choose wisely. They're not baby-dolls that can be put down until we feel like playing grown-up or a rescued animal that can be returned if it doesn't work out.

The list could be exhaustive and there would still be questions and an even deeper search for answers. The former takes minimal energy, the latter takes hard work. Both have great value, but they cannot be independent of each other if we want success. I'd like to end by saying "Its normal for our feelings, actions, and thoughts to be connected to our emotions that what makes us who we are. Without them we'd be robots or machines and it wouldn't matter what happens to us. But, we are matter, living matter, and we are God's concern and so it is and has been for all the generations of mankind before us, as it will be after we are gone from our earthly life.

Take life and take it with care, heal the very heart that you've been created to have and know the hope you have in Christ. Look at a child's face; it's an open book, innocent, fragile and sweet. Their tiny undeveloped features hold the image of the face you see in the mirror. Take the adult away and search for the child; hold it, forgive it, embrace it, and be an adult willing to help it find a better way.

"Can a woman forget her nursing child, and not have compassion on the son of her womb? Surely they may forget, yet I (God) will not forget you." Isaiah49:15

Food for Thought:

- Be gentle with yourself, especially during times of recovery and grieving.
- Ask God to help you during times of need, change, and loss.
- Remember, denial is breeding ground for behaviors that are codependent: like trying to control others, and neglecting ourselves. People in our lives won't change until we change.
- Illness, compulsive and addictive behaviors can take root when we deny we need help.
- Denial doesn't mean something doesn't exist.
- The shame is not in needing help - it's in not getting it!
- Don't let other people's problems, desires and wants set the course for your life.
- Not every person in our life will want to come on our journey, especially when it stops their dysfunctional behaviors, and thinking.

- We are no longer victims when it comes to our repeated poor choices.

- As adults we are responsible for showing others how they can treat us.

- Through our journey of personal recovery, as much as we may want to hold onto the "others" who have been in our lives, or harmed us; until we realize at the end of any given day it comes down to just God, and us.

- The battle to freedom from the past will be much harder, if we expect our abusers to help. It's rare to have our offenders participate in the reconstruction, and healing of our identity, and self worth.

- Discover your own truth. We must stand in our own light in order to get out of the darkness.

- We have to stop letting our happiness be something that someone else holds in their hands. More often than not, it is just an illusion; when we try to make some else responsible for stopping our pain.

- Acceptance of ourselves, and surrender to God moves us forward. Forcing situations and people that are not good for us, does not work.

- Children are gifts, if we accept them. –Kathleen Turner Crilly. This is to include ourselves.

- The issue needs to be whether we care about ourselves or not. Not if we can see, hear or feel whether or not others care. Today start caring about yourself, and taking responsibility for your pain and problems.

- We are not the first to face hard challenges; nor will we be the last. And so goes life, and the common struggles that come to all who live.

- *Therefore humble yourselves under the mighty hand of God, that He may exalt you in proper time, casting all your anxiety on Him, because He cares for you. Be of sober spirit, be on the alert. Your adversary, the devil, prowls around like a roaring lion, seeking someone to devour. But resist him, firm in your faith, knowing that the same experiences of suffering are being accomplished by your brethren who are in the world. After you have suffered for a little while, the God of all grace, who called you to His eternal glory in Christ, will Himself, perfect, confirm, strengthen and establish you. To Him, be power and dominion forever and ever. Amen (1Peter5- 11)*

One of the philosophies that I live by is, "If what has been done to me (us), did not feel good, then what would make me (us), think it will feel any better when I (we) do it to someone else?" The details most assuredly will vary, but the end result is very close in heartache and pain.

- What you compromise you lose.
- People who live defensively never rise above average.
- Having a bad life requires just as much energy as having a good one.
- If you are always looking for offense, you'll find it.
- Keep conflicts impersonal, fight the issues not people.

- What you are looking for is usually at your own house.
- Spiritual strength comes from what you obey, not what you believe.

How much judgment do you really have? In Matthew 7:1-2 says; DO NOT judge and criticize and condemn (others unfairly with an attitude of self-righteous superiority as though assuming the office of a judge), so that you will not be judged (unfairly). 2. "For just as you (hypocritically) judge others (when you are sinful and unrepentant), so will you be judged; and in accordance with your standard of measure (used to pass out judgment), judgment will be measured to you.

THE TRAP OF JUDGEMENT

A church was in need of a pastor. One of the elders was interested in knowing what kind of minister they desired. He wrote a letter of interest and presented it to the pulpit committee as if it had come from an applicant.

Gentlemen:

Understanding that your pulpit is vacant, I would like to apply for the position. I have many qualifications, I think you would appreciate. I have been blessed to preach with power and have some success as a writer. Some say that I am a good organizer. I have been the leader in most of the places I've gone.

However, some folks have some things against me. I am over fifty years of age, and I have never preached in one place for more than three years at a time. In some places I had to leave town, after my work caused riots and disturbances. I have to admit that I have been in jail three or four times but not because of any real wrong doing. My health isn't too good, though I can still get a good deal done.

I have had to work at my trade to help pay my way. The churches I've preached in have been small, but located in several large cities. I have not gotten along well with religious leaders in different towns where I've preached. In fact, some of them have threatened me, taken me to court and even attacked me physically.

I am not too good at keeping records. I have been known to forget those I have baptized. However, if you can use me I will do my best for you, even if I have to work to help with my support.

The elder read this letter to the committee and asked them if they were interested in the applicant. They replied. "He would never do for their church. They were not interested in an unhealthy, contentious, trouble - making, absent minded, ex-jailbird. In fact they felt insulted that his application had been presented."

The committee then asked the name of the applicant, whereupon the elder answered, "THE APOSTLE PAUL."

THOUGHTS TO PONDER

- When we camouflaged judgment as an opinion or observation, we are treading on thin ice. As Jesus said to Peter in JOHN 21:22 "If I want him to remain until I come." Jesus answered, "What is that to you? As for you, follow me."

- Grow a wise heart – you'll do yourself and those that really matter a favor.
- Make a habit of not discussing, looking for and analyzing what isn't there.
- Assumptions are costly and a horrid price to pay, especially when they are made about us!
- Many of us judge because of fear, or because if what we don't understand.
- Judgment comes easy, especially when we have no personal experience in what we are judging.
- It's can be easy for some people to say what they would do, but all the harder sometimes for the person in the trenches doing it.
- It's wise to remember we are accountable for ourselves, and others are accountable for themselves.
- Remembering ways we've grown and changed, should remind us that others are hopefully doing the same.
- Judgment is a form of control. It's not our job to try, and control people or circumstances based on our opinion.
- As Jesus said to Peter when he was overly concerned about what was happening with another disciple, "What's it to you?"
- The only One who has the right to judge, He who is without sin, Jesus. He himself took your judgment on,

so you could walk scot-free. Nobody can judge you once you become saved. You are a new person in Christ and a redeemed child of a King.

THE POWER OF FORGIVENESS

I know I have found it harder to forgive, especially when the hurt has come from someone I loved deeply. Or, when I've been betrayed by or abused by someone I should have been able to trust. Forgiveness doesn't always come easily, but when we read the true life account of Corey Ten Boom; her example should convict us to deal with feelings and experiences that need resolution and often forgiveness.

Corey and her family helped Jews escape the Nazi Holocaust during World War two and saved nearly 800 lives. After Corey watched her sister, Betsie's example of love and forgiveness while they were enduring extreme cruelty, and persecution in the German concentration camps; Corey decided to travel around the world preaching forgiveness and the need for reconciliation.

THOUGHTS TO PONDER

- The person who has the most to gain from forgiveness is the person doing it.
- Forgiveness is the ability to forgive those who have hurt you in anyway. It doesn't mean you want to have dinner with them or spend the rest of your life with them. It means that you release the bitterness in your heart for what they have done.

- "If the world hates you, keep in mind that it hated Me (Jesus) first. If you belonged to the world, it would love you as its own. As it is, you do not belong to the world, but I have chosen you out of the world. That is why the world hates you." John 15:18-19

- Remember what really matters, is what happens in us, not to us. Forgiveness left unchecked will cause physical and emotional ailments, we otherwise would not have had.

- Un-forgiveness is like drinking poison, and expecting the other person to die.

- Don't expect that the person(s) responsible for hurting you will always provide some form of restitution or a remorseful apology.

- None of us want to have enemies, but it's inevitable. The catch is not to have any enemies, but to act differently towards them then the world would have us act.

- The only way to cope with un-forgiveness is to bow your head and ask the Lord to grant you the power to start the process of peeling off the layers of hurt.

- Don't be a martyr. We don't need to prove our pain by holding on to hurt. There is no reward or award for suffering longer, better or more.

- When we don't forgive ourselves, we keep suffering over, and over again the same loss and agony. This is what the foot of the Cross is all about, we leave it there. However, it's also where I offender(s) have the privilege to leave theirs as well.

- Forgiveness doesn't mean it never happened or doesn't hurt. It means we've released ourselves from the enslavement of unhealthy agony.

- *The Lord supports the humble, but He brings the wicked down into the dust. (Psalm 147:6)*

- It takes humility to forgive. Humility is not thinking less of your-self, it's thinking of your-self less.

The Past: Memories and lessons learned.

The Future: Gives hope and dreams to look forward to.

The Present: Gives us something tangible to embrace.

THE BUILDERS

By Henry Wadsworth Longfellow

ALL are architects of fate. Working in these walls of Time;
Some with massive deeds and great.
Some with ornaments of rhyme.

Nothing useless is, or low;
   Each thing in its place is best;
And what seems but idle show
   Strengthens and supports the rest.

For the structure that we raise;
   Time is with materials filled;
Our to-days and yesterdays
   Are the blocks with which we build.

Truly shape and fashion these;
   Leave no yawning gaps between;
Think not, because no man sees,
   Such things will remain unseen.

In the elder days of Art,
   Builders wrought with greatest care,
Each minute and unseen part;
   For the Gods see everywhere.

Let us do our work as well,
   Both the unseen and seen;
Make the house, where Gods may dwell,
   Beautiful, entire and clean.

Else our lives are incomplete,
   Standing in these walls of Time,
Broken stairways, where the feet
   Stumble as they seek to climb.

Build to-day, then strong and sure,
   With a firm and ample base;
And ascending and secure

Shall to-morrow find its place.

Thus alone can we attain
    To those turrets, where the eye
Sees the world as one vast plain,
    And one boundless reach of sky.

SECTION FOUR

Cultivating Faith

God Is Who He Says He Is

Jesus with Children

A Snap Shot of the Big Picture

After people read my life story, I have been asked many times, "How can you or how did you believe there's a God?" My first response is, "How do you or I know there isn't?" Without fail the next question is, "If there is, then why do you think that persons like you, and others have had bad things happen to them? Why do babies get sick and die? Why do innocent people get killed, get diseases? Why are there so wars, and so much pain in the world? Why do bad things happen to good people, and if God is so good then He lets everyone into heaven, right?"

My answer is this: "First of all, you have to start out with a basic belief that He does exist. For most people this is relatively easy. For those who lack this base-line belief, my answer is, "Then why blame someone for the ills of the world, whom you don't believe exists, and if you don't or can't believe in anyone or anything greater than yourself, you're pretty much doomed to do it all on your own anyway." Why do I say doomed? Think about this for just one minute, who do some of the staunch deniers of God call out to when their lives are falling apart? The pleas to God are incredible when fear and agony loom larger than life.

My next answer is, "Read Genesis, it was never God's intention for the suffering, loss, and pain that we humans experience here on the planet earth." Why then did he allow the serpent? This serpent (the devil) was one of God's most beautiful chosen angels. Yet he was dissatisfied with his position in God's creation, just like many of us. Just like this angel Lucifer, God created us (mankind) and angels to resemble Him, unlike plants, and animals. We were blessed with **Free Will** which is one of the greatest expressions of God's love. Think about this for a moment: would you go to a store and purchase a machine or a robot to love or marry, have children with, to nurture you and fellowship with? Would you want to spend your life with an inanimate object, that doesn't care if you're alive or dead and has no emotions that can connect to you?

Free Will: is the ability to choose between different possible courses of action unimpeded. Free will is closely linked to the concepts of moral responsibility, praise, guilt, sin, and other judgments which apply only to actions that are freely chosen. Wikipedia

So, if we are created by God to love, feel, connect, and express these things to each other, why wouldn't He who created us in His image desire these experiences. We would not want to be forced to love or spend our quality intimate time with someone that does not appeal to us? If not then why would God want a forced relationship with us? I'm going to leave my solid and comforting belief here, and let you, the individual reader, to read God's Word, the Bible. And search for the truth that He has for each one of our lives in relation to Him. Because all that matters is your personal relationship and journey with Him. It's your love story.

The Following is the truth(s) through Scripture that I've experienced; prayers that have illuminated my path and thoughts to ponder. They have served me and have strengthened my relationship with God the Father, and our Savior, Jesus Christ. It is my hope and prayer they are a light to you as well.

- *(Psalm 8:3-9) When I consider Your heavens, the work of Your fingers, The moon and stars, which You ordained; what is man that You take thought of him, And the son of man that You care for him? Yet You have made him a little lower than God, And You crown him with glory and majesty! You make him rule over the works of Your hands; You have put all things under his feet, All sheep and oxen, And also the beasts of the field, The birds of the heavens and the fish of the sea, Whatever passes through the paths of the seas, O Lord, our Lord, How majestic is Your name in all the earth!*

- Never become discouraged even if you are to fall more frequently because of your failings; rather get up again, and again with humility and trust. Remember that whatever unsettles you does not come from God but from the devil, who would like us to become despondent so to ensnare us. Get up promptly; once you have fallen, asking pardon of God. Then resume your work / life calmly, with the same trust and courage, as if you had never fallen. We will always have weakness of character, but with good will we can do more than we ever thought possible. With all our faults and failings, we should strive to be gently, humble and patient. Do not be discouraged rather put your trust in God who is the best of fathers. *By Sister Marie Joseph*

- *(Psalm 9:10) And those who know Your name will put their trust in You, For You, O Lord have not forsaken those who seek You.*

- *(Proverbs 24:3) By wisdom a house is built, And by understanding it is established.*

- Trials should give us greater trust in God, more fervor and courage. The more upset we are, the more we should turn to prayer. For it is there we will draw comfort and strength. God's grace will sustain you.

- Do not live indifferent to salvation. Rather let the desire for heaven be on your mind which is the way to draw the loving mercy of God upon you.

- *(Proverbs 16:32) Better to be patient than powerful; better to have self-control than to conquer a city.*

- Your conscience is your inner voice that goes with you through life. It's usually cultivated through our parents, culture and the knowledge of the Bible. When we strive to be devoted to God, our conscience is guided by Holy Spirit and fed through the word.

- *(Romans12:16) Live in harmony with each other. Don't be too proud to enjoy the company of ordinary people. And don't think you know it all!*

- God doesn't only set boundaries in nature, but also for His children. Living beyond God's boundaries is an illusion that you will be free.

- God's heart is open to you through the blood of Jesus Christ. *(Ephesians 3:12) Because of Christ and our faith in Him, we can now come boldly and confidently into God's presence.*

- Choose your advisors carefully and consult those who make wise decisions. *(Proverbs 13:10) Pride leads to conflict; those who take advice are wise.*

- *(Daniel 6:21-22) Daniel answered, "My God sent His angel, and He shut the mouths of the lions. They have not hurt me, because I was found innocent in His sight. Angels were created by God to serve Him and be under His authority. You don't honor or worship them, because He created them. But, God has equipped them with tremendous powers and they are His army to do His will. (Psalms34:7) For He will command His angels concerning you to guard you in all your ways.*

- *(Psalm 27:10) even though my father and mother abandon me, the Lord will hold me close.* For three long agonizing hours the world became dark, as Jesus the Son of God cried out, "My God, why have You, forsaken me?" For the first time he was separated and not one with the Father. The Father let all the sin of the world rest on His shoulders, and in this time of separation, Jesus tore the temple curtain so that we could have access without separation to the Father. (*John 14:18*) "*I will not abandon you as orphans – I will come to you.*"

- Silence helps lift the soul to God, it is in silence that God makes His voice heard and speaks to the heart.

- We do not have to believe in God or the Bible, but we're all going to be judged by them some day. If we don't believe then what are we living by and what will we die by?

- Wouldn't it better to believe that God and heaven are real, than to die, and find out we were wrong. (*John 11:25-29) Jesus answered them, "I told you, and you do not believe; works that I do in My Father's name, these testify of me. But you do not believe because you are not of My Sheep. My sheep hear My Voice, and I know them, and they follow me; and I give eternal life to them, and they will not perish; and no one will snatch them out of My hand, My Father, who has given them to Me, is greater than all; and no one is able to snatch them out of the Father's hand.*

- *In (1 Kings 3:16-28) Solomon Wisely Judges.* I love this Scripture and it has enabled me to be a better mother to my children. When you read this Scripture you're inclined to think it's all about Solomon's wise judgment. Actually for me nothing could be further from the truth. Not that he wasn't wise, he was. I see the sacrificial heart of the real mother of the living child. Her love for the baby's life superseded her need to have what was rightfully hers! While the other woman would have rather seen the child cut in half instead of accepting the fact that hers had died. Tragically this woman was unable to have any compassion for the mother of the living child.

- *What good is it for someone to gain the whole world, yet forfeit their soul?(Mark 8:36)*

- *People who long to be rich fall into temptation and are trapped by many foolish and harmful desires that plunge them into ruin and destruction.(1 Timothy 6:9)*

- We live in a broken world, and suffering is part of life. Sometimes we get answers to our questions and other times we don't. We feel like Job, we want to throw ourselves on the ground, and can feel nothing but our agony. During this time we can cry out to God; our emotions and tears secrete chemicals in our brains that help us to feel better. This is why knowledge, of Him who creates us, even when we cannot understand, will give us peace that surpasses all understanding.

- *After we have suffered a little while, the God of all grace will Himself restore you. (1 Peter 5:10) We rejoice in our sufferings, knowing that suffering produces endurance, and endurance produces character, and character produces hope, and hope does not put us to shame, because God's love has been poured into our hearts through the Holy spirit who has been given to us. (Romans:3-5)*

The following is not original to me I received it several years ago on a bookmark from Dr. David Jeremiah from Turning Point Ministries:

Mercy & Grace

Mercy withholds the knife from the heart of Isaac

Grace provides a ram in the thicket

Geneses 22:11-14

Mercy runs to forgive the prodigal

Grace throws a party with a robe, a ring and a fatted calf.

Luke 15:20-24

Mercy hears the cry of the thief on the cross

Grace promises paradise that very day

Luke 23:39-43

Mercy converts Paul on the road to Damascus

Grace call him to be the great apostle

Acts 9:1-6, 17

Mercy closes the door to hades

Grace opens the door to heaven

Ephesians 2:8-9

And the difference between Mercy and Grace is this –

Mercy – withholds from us what we deserve

Grace – gives us want we do not deserve

Romans 5:20

SECTION FIVE

Afterword and the 11th Hour

Whether it is obvious to us or not, we're all living in the 11th hour of our lives. There isn't a dawn of a new day, the dark of night, or a second that passes that we aren't walking in the 11th hour of our life. Not another person's hour, but our own. It will serve us well to think on this sobering reality, at least once in a 24-hour period. Like our relationship with God, we tend to get complacent about life and take for granted what lies ahead or even in the next few minutes and hours.

But of that day and hour no one knows, not even the angels of heaven, nor the Son of man, but the Father alone (Matthew 24:36).

Take heed, keep on the alert, for you do not know when the appointed time will come (Mark 13:13).

We seem to fall into a false sense of security, much like using credit cards. We must be able to afford it, because we have been entrusted to use our "free will" (remember this in our relationship with God), to have the availability to spend which we in reality, often do not have! We have feelings of boundless limitation. Often we deceive ourselves into the lie that we can afford the luxury, and spontaneity of the moment. It's akin to with different details, "I will think about eternity, God, Jesus and if heaven is real tomorrow." So, we end up

142

shelving the reality of our need to decision for another month, year or decade. But, what if tomorrow comes? Today, tonight or in the next few hours, there are no more tomorrows left?

You lose your job, your health or a disaster strikes; and the debt of false security is still due, then what? What if you get a phone call that your loved one was killed in an accident or died from an unexpected heart-attack? Better yet, what if it's you? While I'm not advocating for people to live in constant fear, and always looking their shoulder or someone else's; what I am saying is, "It's wise to be aware and understand the things that matter most." Example like for every swipe of a credit card there will be a payday. This one is very personal to me. As I sit penning this book, I am a hostage to credit card debt, which I've accumulated through generosity, fear, temporary emotional relief, and compensation to others which I did not owe, and I did not have the ability to do or pay for. It has cost me financially, spiritually, and relationally.

The rich rule over the poor, and the borrower is a slave to the lender (Proverbs 22:7).

Whenever we live in the passion of the moment, fill a need, dull a pain or try deal to fix another person's life by spending and living beyond our means; we are destined to hear the clock strike beyond the 11th hour, because our debt will come due! However, if we have enough faith and fortitude, through sincere repentance and accountability we can dig ourselves out of this self-imposed prison a little at a time. And with God's grace, we will start to see the light again. One might ask, "Why would someone choose to expose this about themselves?" For me the journey has been hard, but the answer is quite simple. It is not for fame, fortune, sympathy, or attention; but for God's sake. In all honesty, these things all have come into play on some level in one way or another, and for many different reasons. However, when you have no agenda but to honor God by being transparent, I believe especially when your motive is to enrich the lives of others; it is one of the greatest expressions of our love not only for Him, but also for them. It's an act of unhindered and unexpected love to be humble enough to show your weakness in the world and your strength in Christ.

These things I have spoken to you, so that in Me you may have peace. In the world you have tribulation, but take courage; I have overcome the world (John 16: 33).

As far as the 11th hour in life, death, and relational realities, we're talking about something very different. There are many unexpected points of no return. This should be as sobering as it sounds to us all. I will not put God in a box and I am not privy to anyone's last breath, including my own. What I do know for certain is that it will come and is inescapable for the human race. Only God knows who is lost and who is saved, and only He alone can change that final moment when the last heartbeat sounds and the final breath is drawn. It's a fate that we can participate in through grasping the reality of God as our Creator and heaven as our eternal destination, acquired only through Christ as our Savior and intercessor to God the Father.

In this the 11th hour of human life there is rarely a warning alarm, only for those diagnosed with a terminal illness. It's then that the grace of God, even in the face of such sorrowful realities, we are afforded the time to choose heaven or hell. For those who say, "They've never talked to or seen anyone who's been there, so they don't know if it's real or not," I would say to them, "Wouldn't it be far better to believe in God and Jesus as your Savior; and heaven as your eternal home, than to die and find out you were wrong?"

...Otherwise, Christ would have had to suffer repeatedly since the foundation of the world. But now He has appeared once for all at the end of the ages to do away with sin by the sacrifice of Himself. ***Just as man is appointed to die once, and after that to face judgment,*** *so also Christ was offered once to bear the sins of many; and He will appear a second time, not to bear sin, but to bring salvation to those who eagerly await him (Hebrews 9: 26-28).* I try to live knowing my hours and days are limited, not only to do what I can while I still have the life and desire to accomplish things, but rather to be mindful of my relationship with God and the unknown hour of my death.

Relationally and in other serious life events, we may cheat someone else, in many ways or out of many things before we have our day of reckoning, but it will come. The strangest thing about this is that people will often get the return on their "investment" (what they've given or done), in a way that may be very different from what they did to someone else; and often in a more painful emotionally, physically or financial way. And in disbelief, without a thought of their own actions, they wonder why? The Bible is clear on the reaping and sowing principal, we use this principal all the time even those aren't believers. You know the Golden Rule, we want what we give. Or do we? In many areas of life we have a preset conception of what we expect from another person or situation in our lives, except when it comes to the poor choices we make that hurt or rob others.

Be not deceived; God is not mocked; for whatsoever a man sows, this he will also reap. For the one who sows to his own flesh shall of the flesh will from the flesh reap corruption, but he the one who sows to the Spirit will from the Spirit reap eternal life. (Galatians 6:7-8).

It's well worth pondering what we would like our 11th hour to look like. Where do we want to be; who do we want to be with here and after the clock strikes 12? How do we want to spend our time and money? Is it all about the here and now or do we care about the days and few months or years ahead? I believe we should live pondering and reflecting as much as possible; it's during these times we can have the scales removed from our eyes, and just sit with what is, what has been, and what could be.

The Handwriting on the Wall

August 2020

Blessed is the nation whose God is the Lord, The people whom He has chosen for His own inheritance. (Psalm 33:12)

God reigns over the nations, God sits on His holy throne. (Psalm 47:8)

Your kingdom is an everlasting kingdom, And Your dominion endures throughout all generations. (Pslam145:13)

But the Lord abides forever; He established His throne for judgment. And he will judge the world in righteousness; He will execute judgment for the peoples with equity.

(Psalm 9:7-8)

You, o Lord, rule forever; Your throne is from generation to generation. (Lamentations 5:19)

Then the seventh angel sounded; and there were loud voices in heaven saying, "the kingdom of the world has become the kingdom of our Lord and His Christ; and He will reign forever and ever." (Revelation 11:15)

The climate of the culture in which we are living right now is an experience the present generation might feel is the worst it's ever been; as it has been with past generations, and will be with those to come. The human race is sorrowful, great, depraved, and exquisite all at the same time. The political and religious divide we're living in is pitting people from all walks of life against each other. Adult bullies are more common than school bullies, and in every arena of life. Compassion and forethought are rare at best, and if anyone gets in anyone's way they had better watch out. Nothing is off limits across the board.

Sibling against sibling, parents against their children and vise versa. Longtime friends, neighbors, co-workers, business owners, and customers are walking away from each other after decades of loyalty. It almost seems that regardless of where you go now, you are amongst strangers. Our lives have become overshadowed with an eerie sense of distrust and uncertainty. Science and the social media are cashing in on fears that prey on the human mind; causing many people to willingly submit to the orders of the day. At the same time freewill is running roughshod with evil that permeates our society. Faith, trust, and hope in our divine Creator is fading fast, even among professing Christians.

We seem to be exchanging the reality of dying once, and facing after this the judgment seat of God, for unbridled restraint to satisfy the lustfulness of our human nature. Living any way we choose and ignoring the effect it has on God and those around us. Like a tsunami striking our country, many people are promoting ill-gotten gains, immorality, and worshiping false idols. And many want to deny that the fiery gates of hell exist, so they trough caution to the wind, and give no thought of life beyond the moment. This year I have seen Christians turn on Christians and in one fell-swoop make a mockery of their lifelong testimony; because the ego superseded humility at the foot of the cross.

Those screaming for social justice and tolerance often disguised as advocates have the least tolerance of all. Many seem to excuse themselves from any level of accountability or adherence to the standard for which they themselves have set for others. Any differing views may be met with anger, verbal or physical abuse, the destruction of one's life, home or business; nothing is off limits. And those who disagree with them cannot cower low enough to satisfy them; nothing short of absolutely forgoing your views and beliefs is acceptable.

The truth has been distorted and couched and camouflaged to cover up lies, cheating and perversion. A lie is now the succulent utopia of the moment and new way of thinking and living. The skeletons that people dig out of another person's closet, is more often than not, presented through a thick haze of smoke and mirrors to serve the persons or purpose at hand; because after all, "it is the end that justifies the means?" Innocent people and the very fabric of our nation getting destroyed does not seem to enter the equation. On the sidelines are the minority: strivers and survivors, trying not to lose heart, who work not just for themselves, but for the good of all. And no society would be complete without those who continue to be victims of their own poor choices, with the "I Can't" mindset.

I shudder when I think about people who do not have a healthy sense of respect and fear of God, authority, and loss of freedom. While we've seen abuse of authority this year, as in years past; we've seen a greater disgrace of "Americans" taking to the streets, and acting ten times worse than those they accuse! Those who don't seem to see this atrocity, is starting to far out- number those who do. So where does one put their trust: in a spouse, a friend, a doctor, family or a leader of some sort? On any given day you wake up and go to sleep alone, except for God, who gave you the very breath you breathe, both day and night. He my friends, is the only One we can really trust.

How many times over the years have we told ourselves or someone else, "I would never do this or that?" Who is one hundred percent sure how they'll cross a certain bridge until we are across it? There is always another side to every situation, and another side to every person. There is not always another way over the bridge, unless we forgo the trip entirely. Especially in today's social environment, we are challenged with choices in ways some of us would have never dreamed of. As reverend Danny Jones from Northlake Baptist Church says, "It's not what are we going to do, but what are you going to do?" God bless this man, for this is one of the truest statements ever spoken.

In a few short months from finalizing this manuscript, the upheaval of another presidential election for these United States of America will be fast underway; and only God knows as before, and in the times ahead, what kind strife and challenges His children will inflict on one another. However, His sovereignty is rock solid and unchangeable over all that happens, and us. He will not be mocked, moved, or bought for any price. For God has paid the price of all prices for your soul and mine with His Son, the Lord Jesus Christ.

Take heart and take it lightly more on some days, and a little more seriously on others, because it's there that we can find harmony and the balance we need to endure. May you find the time to hone and prepare for your 11th hour, and may God's grace be sufficient to help you along the way.

Thank you for allowing me into a small corner of your world to share a small corner of mine. Only God knows what lies ahead, but this I do know: To God we are beautiful, loved, precious, strong, protected, empowered, and chosen.

Blessings Always,

Colleen L. Bruce

Made in the USA
Monee, IL
03 October 2020